PLAIN
TALK
ON

Revelation

BOOKS BY DR. GUTZKE . . .

Plain Talk About Christian Words
Plain Talk on Acts
Plain Talk on Luke
Plain Talk on Matthew
Plain Talk on John
Plain Talk on James
Plain Talk on Ephesians
Plain Talk on Exodus
Plain Talk on Genesis
Plain Talk on Mark
Plain Talk on Philippians
Plain Talk on Hebrews
Plain Talk on Romans
Plain Talk on Isaiah
Plain Talk on the Epistles of John
Plain Talk on Corinthians
Plain Talk on Galatians
Plain Talk on Timothy, Titus, and Philemon
Plain Talk on Peter and Jude
Plain Talk on Revelation
Plain Talk on Deuteronomy
Plain Talk on Thessalonians
Plain Talk on the Minor Prophets
Plain Talk on Leviticus and Numbers
Plain Talk on Colossians

PLAIN TALK ON

Revelation

MANFORD GEORGE GUTZKE
PH.D.

ZONDERVAN
PUBLISHING HOUSE OF THE ZONDERVAN CORPORATION
GRAND RAPIDS, MICHIGAN 49506

Library of Congress Cataloging in Publication Data
Gutzke, Manford George, 1896-
    Plain talk on Revelation.

    1. Bible. N.T. Revelation—Commentaries. I. Title
BS2825.3.G8   228'.07   79-15010
ISBN 0-310-25681-X

Printed in the United States of America

83   84   85   86   87   88 — 10   9   8   7

CONTENTS

Chapter 1 7
Chapter 2 25
Chapter 3 56
Chapter 4 64
Chapters 5 and 6 73
Chapter 7 85
Chapters 8 and 9 90
Chapters 10, 11, and 12 97
Chapters 13 and 14 106
Chapter 15 119
Chapter 16 124
Chapter 17 131
Chapter 18 141
Chapters 19 and 20 147
Chapters 21 and 22 166

Chapter 1

† † †

BLESSING IS PROMISED
(Revelation 1:1-3)

The Book of Revelation talks about something that from beginning to end occurred in heaven. In it we look through the eyes of the apostle John to see things in heaven. What man on earth knows enough to understand what all those things mean? Or what man is worthy to speak of those things? In our present condition, in this human body of ours, we are not fit to walk into that presence. Only holy beings are there, as we learn in Revelation, but you and I are given permission to look into it.

God has graciously revealed to us certain things that He will use to bless our souls. He wants you and me here on earth to be conscious of the inward glory of His very presence. He knows we live in this world "like it is." He knows all the mundane features of living down here on earth—the dust and the mud that lie about us. God knows about that. But He wants our hearts to be conscious of Him, and so in His great grace He reveals to us in His Word and in the face of Jesus Christ that which belongs to Him. The revelation is for us. And He wants us to look up and, looking up, to be lifted into His very presence.

You will notice the title "The Revelation." Now, the traditional title in the King James Version is "The Revelation of St. John the Divine," but that is not part of the inspired record. That name was given by the early compilers of the Scripture. But we get the real idea in the very first verses of the first chapter.

> The Revelation of Jesus Christ, which God gave unto him, to show unto his servants things which must shortly come to pass;

7

and he sent and signified it by his angel unto his servant John:
Who bare record of the word of God, and of the testimony of
Jesus Christ, and of all things that he saw (1:1-2).

These two verses relate John's account of what this book is,
how it came to be, and what it is about. "The Revelation of
Jesus Christ." We are supposed to see something in this. This
is the unveiling of Jesus Christ. As much as we look into it,
and however far beyond us we feel these things are, we are
intended to learn about the Lord Jesus Christ in this book.

"The Revelation of Jesus Christ, which God gave unto
him." God the Father gave to the Lord Jesus Christ this
revelation to be shared with His church. "To show unto his
servants" leads us to say at the outset that this book is obviously for believing people. As we get further into the book,
we can understand why this is so; but we are to recognize at
the outset that this is something God gave to the Lord Jesus
Christ to show unto His servants. Actually the people of the
world, unbelieving people, would not be interested in what is
in this Book of Revelation. But for His people, those who
believe in Him, this is special; it is for them.

The Lord wants believers to see these things: things which
must shortly come to pass. I am not sure the phrase "shortly
come to pass" has any chronology implicit in it or any time
schedule about it. I think it is much the same as when John
the Baptist was preaching and said, "The kingdom of heaven
is at hand." He meant this to say, "It is now operative and will
be real right now." The revelation of Jesus Christ which believers are to see, which God gave unto the Lord to show unto
His servants, is a revelation of things which are now operative
and becoming actual and real. "Must shortly come to pass"
means to say nothing will ever prevent their happening. Actually God is operating in them now.

"And he sent and signified it by his angel." That word
"signified" implies "showed it by signs." He signified it by His
angel unto His servant John. He signified these things which
are to come to pass through signs that He manipulated and
showed to John.

Let us consider how it is with signs. When you see a post
with a sign "Adams Park," everyone knows that isn't Adams
Park; that is just a sign pointing to Adams Park. Anytime you

see a sign, it gives you a name and points in a certain direc-
tion, but it is not the thing itself. So when we see signs that
are mentioned in this book, we will notice them, but at the
same time we will say to ourselves, "These signs are intended
to direct our attention to the truth." As much as I can, I will
share with you what I think the truth is toward which these
signs point.

"And he sent and signified it by his angel unto his servant
John." The meaning of the phrase "by his angel" remains
obscure to us. It refers to someone whom He sent, some
messenger that He used to bring this truth across to John.
Later on in the book John mentions the angel again and tells
what the angel said. Some angels are described in the Bible
and some are not. In Revelation, John uses the word "angel"
without description.

No angel is described in specific terms in the Bible. The
term "angel" has more to do with the function than with the
descriptive appearance. On one occasion angels may be
clothed with white garments; on another, angels may look like
human beings; on still another occasion, angels are not described at all. We remember that when the women came to
the tomb after Jesus' resurrection, they saw two men with
white garments (Luke 24). We remember that when the
disciples were standing there looking up into the heavens
after the Lord Jesus ascended, two men with white garments
came and spoke to them (Acts 1). But when Gideon was
threshing wheat on his father's farm and a messenger, an
angel, met him and asked him for food, apparently there
wasn't anything about the appearance of that being that struck
Gideon as being extraordinary (Judg. 6). But it was an angel.

Once three angels came to Abraham's tent. Abraham entertained them as if they were human beings, apparently not
knowing that he had thereby "entertained angels unawares."
He went out and killed a kid and dressed it. Then Sarah
prepared a meal for these persons, who were afterwards
called angels (Gen. 18; Heb. 13:2). Thus we can see that the
word "angel" refers more to function than to description.

* * *

John identifies himself in the second verse: "Who bare record of the word of God, and of the testimony of Jesus Christ, and of all things that he saw." This does not mean there were three separate bodies of data. Nor does it mean that the Word of God forms one part of the book, the testimony of Jesus Christ, another part of the book; and finally all the things that he saw, another part of the book. It is not that way. Consider it like this: John bore record of the Word of God, and that was the testimony of Jesus Christ, which is in the Word of God; and that was all things that he saw, which was the testimony of Jesus Christ. The whole Book of Revelation is one connected revelation. From the beginning to the end, it is one vision that John had.

> Blessed is he that readeth, and they that hear the words of this prophecy, and keep those things which are written therein: for the time is at hand (1:3).

It has often been said that this is the one book in the Bible in which we are promised a blessing if we read it. We are promised a blessing if we even hear it read. But I think that the hearing includes thinking some about it. The Bible says, "He that hath an ear to hear, let him hear." This means much more than just letting the words come into our ears. We are to think about what has been said.

"And keep those things which are written therein." We should not miss that sentence, that clause, because I am inclined to think that what John was sharing here with the churches has a certain implication in it. There is a certain call to the hearer, as there is in all the Word of God. God does not reveal anything that does not call us to Himself along the lines of His revelation. We keep those things when we cherish them. We remember them. What we keep in this connection, "keep those things which are written therein," is done in the way we keep a keepsake. This is something that we guard in a special way because we do not want by any chance to lose it.

When we are keeping the commandments of God we call them to mind and cherish them as if they were precious gems. God promises a special blessing upon those who cherish the things of God, who hold them to their hearts. It is the whole wonder of the gospel that God does so much for us. Anyone can have the blessing. There is nothing to do but to receive. All in the world anyone needs is to be empty and then receive and cherish in the heart what God will do. It is to be my privilege in the course of this study to expound the things recorded in such a way that we can see more and more of the glory of what God has prepared for you and for me.

The whole matter of belonging to the Lord Jesus Christ has a tone of victory about it. There is a glory about it. It goes far beyond this world. We live in this world; but we are not altogether of this world. In the Book of Revelation our focus rests on the very presence of God. God is going to deal with us. "Blessed is he that readeth, and they that hear the words of this prophecy, and keep those things which are written therein: for the time is at hand." This verse means to say that these things are now operative. The things we are going to see in this book are working right now.

THE FAITHFUL WITNESS
(Revelation 1:4-7)

The fourth verse of Revelation 1 reads as though this is where John begins.

> John to the seven churches which are in Asia: Grace be unto you, and peace . . . (1:4).

Let us consider something about the "seven churches." There are many "sevens" in the Book of Revelation. In the course of this study we will consider the significance of numbers as well as we can understand it. It has long been held in tradition that the word "seven" is generally associated with a sense of completeness, of totality. When it is used here in referring to the "seven churches" I think it means the whole church on earth. In one of the most important phrases in verse 4 we see that "seven" is mentioned again.

> John to the seven churches which are in Asia: Grace be unto you, and peace, from him which is, and which was, and which is to come; and from the seven Spirits which are before his throne (1:4).

All the scholars I have ever read in this connection seem to feel that when the Scripture reads here "seven Spirits," this does not mean the Holy Spirit and six others. It is taken to mean the sevenfold Holy Spirit of God as mentioned in Isaiah 11:2, where the seven spirits are named: "The Spirit of the Lord" and then other spirits—the spirit of glory, the spirit of justice, and so on. Thus, when we read here "from the seven Spirits which are before his throne," it seems to be a fair interpretation to say, "The Holy Spirit, the total Holy Spirit, which is before the throne of God."

In the same way, the text says, "to the seven churches," this does not mean that the message is limited to only seven congregations. It means to all the church. To "the seven churches" would mean the total church, which is in Asia Minor. However, as happened with any other epistle, the message that was sent to a particular church was always sent through that one to the whole church everywhere.

"Grace be unto you, and peace." Grace is what God brings to man. It is grace that forgives sins. It is grace that changes a person's nature. It is grace that puts into the believer the disposition to do God's will. It is grace that makes the believer rich with the presence of God. It is grace that keeps the believer in the presence of God. Everything that God gives to the believer, to change him, to strengthen him, to comfort him, to keep him, to lead him is of the grace of God. And when the apostle Paul or the apostle John or any other apostle says, "Grace be unto you," it is a prayer. We could express it, "May God share Himself with you graciously," which has in it the promise of what you never deserve but what God in His goodness will give you. So "Grace be unto you [God doing for you], and peace." Peace is something you have; peace is something inside you. Grace is something God gives to you, but peace is something you have in the course of your personal experience.

And notice the threefold source of blessing:

> From him which is, and which was, and which is to come; and from the seven Spirits which are before his throne; and from Jesus Christ, who is the faithful witness, and the first begotten of the dead, and the prince of the kings of the earth (1:4-5).

This means to say, "Grace be unto you and peace from God the Father, the Holy Spirit, and the Lord Jesus Christ." This is a good reference to the Trinity. Blessing is from Him "which is, which was, and which is to come." This does not necessarily refer so much to history as it is a way of describing more fully what is meant by "eternal." One could have said "from Him who is eternal." What do you mean by eternal? Well, He was, and He is, and He will be. Anyone who is acquainted with the original languages of Scripture will recognize that this is the name commonly translated "Jehovah." Some more specifically and technically try to use the word "Yahweh." Either way this is the same name of God that was revealed to Moses. It is a form of the Hebrew verb "to be," which includes all tenses. Different translations disclose that what God revealed to Moses was that He is God from ever and ever, and now, and for ever and ever. He is the God who *had been* with them, the God who *was* with them, and the God who *would be* with them. Some people interpreting that will tell you that what He gave to Moses was the revelation that He was the God who was going to be everything that we would need: that is true. He also is everything that we need: that is true. He also will be everything that we need: that is true. He is the eternal God.

"And from the seven Spirits which are before his throne." "Before His throne" implies "ready to do His will." In the Godhead, God the Father is the executive Head and is the One who directs; the Holy Spirit is the obedient One, the One who goes; and Jesus Christ is the obedient Son, the One who dies. So this blessing was to come from the seven Spirits which are before His throne and from Jesus Christ.

Three things are said about Jesus Christ. "Who is the faithful witness"—He witnesses to the truth, fulfilling His office as a Prophet. "And the first begotten of the dead"—He is the first who rose from the dead to enter into the presence of God and to worship Him, and this is His present High Priestly activity. "And the prince of the kings of the earth"— this is Christ as King. The Scripture sets forth the various offices of Christ as Prophet, Priest, and King.

Thus we see that John begins his message with this salutation: "John to the whole church, Grace be unto you and peace from the Godhead, God the Father, the Son, and the Holy Spirit." And after this salutation, he breaks into praise.

> Unto him that loved us, and washed us from our sins in his own
> blood, and hath made us kings and priests unto God and his
> Father; to him be glory and dominion for ever and ever. Amen
> (1:5-6).

It is as though the apostle could not pass by mentioning Jesus
Christ without paying this tribute to Him. John mentions
three things that Jesus Christ had already done. "Unto him
that loved us"—He showed His love in that He came and
died for us when we were yet sinners. "And washed us from
our sins in his own blood"—this He had done because He
loved us. "And hath made us kings and priests unto God and
his Father"—He has given us a place of service which comes
after we are cleansed. First Jesus loved us, then because He
loved us He cleansed us, and because we were clean He made
us servants of God.

"To him be glory and dominion for ever and ever. Amen."
In this it is as though the apostle—knowing what he would
write in this book, considering how he would tell us about the
revelation of Jesus Christ, and having mentioned His
name—spontaneously exclaims, "O may the name of the Lord
Jesus Christ be glorified for ever and ever beyond everything!" He will say that a number of times in the Book of
Revelation, and he cannot help but say it now.

> Behold, he cometh with clouds; and every eye shall see him,
> and they also which pierced him: and all kindreds of the earth
> shall wail because of him. Even so, Amen (1:7).

John has just told in verses 5 and 6 what Jesus Christ has
done, and now in verse 7 he tells us what Christ is going to do.
When John writes "He cometh with clouds" it reminds us that
in the Gospels the Lord Jesus Himself told Pilate that he
would see the Son of man coming from heaven in clouds of
glory. In 2 Thessalonians it is written that He comes in clouds
of glory with His saints and that He comes into this world to
be beheld by other people. So here "He cometh with clouds"
means to say the Lord is coming in the power and the strength
and the glory of heaven itself. The Lord Jesus Christ is not
finished in this world.

The world knew Jesus Christ as a baby. The world knew
Him as a child and as a young man, and it paid Him no
attention. The world knew Him as a preacher and worker of

wonders and miracles, but still it paid Him no attention. The
world knew Him as one who went about to reveal the things of
God, and it saw Him put to death. But that is as far as the
world could go. Since then, the world has heard the testimony
of His disciples who affirmed that Jesus is alive. No New
Testament writer said He is alive who did not also say that He
is coming back. Every single one of them said it: the Lord
Jesus who is living now in the presence of God is not finished
on this earth. He has not finished His task. We may be
finished when our threescore and ten are done, and we will go
then to be with the Lord. But Jesus is not finished. He is
there in the presence of God interceding on our behalf, praying for us, and waiting God's time. A day is coming when He
will reveal Himself. That is spoken of as the Parousia, when
He will reveal Himself and every eye shall see Him, and they
also that pierced Him. "And all kindreds of the earth shall wail
because of him. Even so, Amen."

This suggests an idea about the coming of the Lord that
believing people ordinarily do not consider. Believers usually
think about what the Lord Jesus is yet going to do—take them
to Himself. We are told not to be alarmed.

> Let not your heart be troubled: ye believe in God, believe also
> in me. In my Father's house are many mansions: if it were not
> so, I would have told you. I go to prepare a place for you. And if
> I go and prepare a place for you, I will come again, and receive
> you unto myself; that where I am, there ye may be also (John
> 14:1-3).

Every believer is hoping one day to see Christ face to face.
We sing, "Face to face, shall I behold Him." Every believer
has in mind that

> When all my labors and trials are o'er,
> And I am safe on that beautiful shore,
> Just to be near the dear Lord I adore
> Will thro' the ages be glory for me.

It is a wonderful expectation, and it is found all through the
Gospels and the Epistles. But here is something revealed to
His servant. The rest of the world is going to know it too—
when He comes. Yet there will be many that wail because of
Him, because the Lord Jesus is coming from the very pres-
ence of God. As we shall see in this book, He will come in

divine power to render judgment upon all who have dis-
obeyed God, even as He comes in mercy and grace to save to
the uttermost everyone who believes in Him.

Having said these two things—first paying tribute in verse
6 to what Christ has done and ending it with "Amen," and
then in verse 7 pointing forward to what He will do—John
ends the passage saying, "Even so, Amen."

JOHN IN PATMOS
(Revelation 1:8-10)

When considering the Book of Revelation, we should keep in
mind that what is seen in the vision is not pictures but symbols. The man who wrote the book was a prisoner on the isle
of Patmos, who called himself John. He wrote at a time when
believers in Christ were under persecution. The government
of the country, namely the Roman government, was persecuting the people who professed faith in Christ Jesus. John
himself was a prisoner, somewhat like an exile.

John wrote these things to believers in Christ, but his
writing had to pass through alien hands, through Roman soldiers' hands. When they read his letter they would be looking
for anything by which they could accuse this prisoner of subversive tendencies. Therefore the truths that John wanted to
convey to these people were put in his writing cryptically.
They were hidden as if one would hide a thing in a cave.

The symbols used by John were known to the believers in
Christ, but were unknown to the Roman soldiers. Thus the
writings of John could slip through the hands of the Roman
soldiers without causing any particular stir. I think many of
the Roman soldiers probably read the Book of Revelation and
felt about it the way many people today feel when they read
the book. It seems to make no sense, they think. And they
say, "Well, anyone who wants to read that stuff, can." That
was the way John got his message through, and that was the
way it could be spread. Even so, when believing people read
what is written with their hearts open to the meaning of those
symbols and to the actual truth revealed in them, their hearts

are greatly lifted and strengthened.

During any time of persecution, any time of disaster, any time of distress, this book is commonly recognized as one of the favorite books in the Bible. In my research I have been amazed to find that, during the history of the church as a whole, in times when people were under special strain and stress they turned most often to Revelation as the book for their private devotional reading. I trust under God that in our study we may catch some little glimpse of why all this was.

Four books in the Bible are written like Revelation. Three in the Old Testament—Ezekiel, Daniel, and Zechariah—and this one in the New Testament are written in symbolic language. Ezekiel was a prisoner at the river Chebar when he wrote his book. Daniel was a prisoner in the city of Babylon when he wrote his book. Zechariah was not exactly a prisoner, but he was returning from Persia and was under a foreign power at the time he wrote his book. And John was on the isle of Patmos, a prisoner, when he wrote his book. Each one of these four books was written at a time when the dominant controlling power was an alien mind, alien to the Scriptures. The authorities were sensitive about anything subversive, ready to kill anyone saying anything against the government. And because the message could be so easily misunderstood, these things were written apparently in this cryptic fashion. I will have something more to say about this, but it will help us to keep in mind that we have not pictures, but symbols.

Let us consider the function of a symbol. The United States of America, as far as the world is concerned, often uses a symbol of an eagle with outstretched wings. That is not the United States of America, but that is a symbol. Just so in the Book of Revelation we find symbols.

> I am Alpha and Omega, the beginning and the ending, saith the Lord, which is, and which was, and which is to come, the Almighty (1:8).

It seems clear from the context, that it does not mean that at this time an audible voice was speaking to John. This is rather John's way of saying something that identifies God. "Alpha and Omega" were the first and last letters of the Greek alphabet. People in America today would say "I am A to Z." Most people know what A to Z means: everything. When a person says "I know everything from A to Z," he means to say he knows the whole business. Here the Lord says "I am A and Z: the first and the last." That is all this means. The Lord in effect states, "In all that is taking place, I am the starter and the stopper of everything there is." This is God.

"The beginning and the ending, saith the Lord, which is, and which was, and which is to come, the Almighty." Here we have the present, the past, and the future. That is one way of getting across to you "everlasting." Or "eternal." Notice who God is. God is the One who started the whole thing and will wind it up. He is from everlasting to everlasting. This is what John emphasizes right at the beginning of his book. When we are dealing with God, we are dealing not with an actor, but with the One who started the whole business, runs the whole business, and winds up the whole business. God has it in His hands. That is what is emphasized at this point.

> I John, who also am your brother, and companion in tribula-
> tion, and in the kingdom and patience of Jesus Christ . . . (1:9).

Now, I think this could be translated to say "in tribulation, and in the patience of Jesus Christ." Notice three things: tribulation, kingdom, and patience.

In almost all the epistles of the New Testament, the writer identifies himself as an apostle. In this case John writes "your brother, and companion." It is interesting, and some students make a point of the fact, that the writer here does not call himself an apostle. But I think this is not too significant. John wanted to share something that came to him. He was a brother and companion with the other believers of his day and time, who were in tribulation and in the kingdom and patience of Jesus Christ. He writes that as they were in tribulation and were suffering persecution at that time, so he also was a prisoner, suffering persecution. They were in the kingdom of Jesus Christ because they accepted the Lord Jesus as their Lord; and they were in the patience of Jesus Christ because they were committed to Him to endure all the way through this life into His very presence.

> I John, who also am your brother, and companion in tribula-
> tion, and in the kingdom and patience of Jesus Christ, was in
> the isle that is called Patmos, for the word of God, and for the
> testimony of Jesus Christ (1:9).

I think that when John expresses his thoughts this way, it is not so much to say "I was in this island in order that I might preach the word and that I might give testimony," as "I was in this island as a prisoner because I preached the word and because I testified to Jesus Christ." That is the way John identifies himself.

> I was in the Spirit on the Lord's day, and heard behind me a great voice, as of a trumpet (1:10).

John's being "in the Spirit" is commonly understood to mean that he was in such a state of communion with the Lord that he himself was caught up in personal fellowship and communion with the Lord through the working of the Holy Spirit in him. It has been suggested that this is very similar to Paul's word in Corinthians when Paul wrote that he spoke of one who was caught up into the third heaven—whether in the body or out of the body, he did not know. But he was in that state of communion and fellowship with Christ. Some people have described this as a kind of ecstasy, as a sort of trance, but all that I think you and I need to read out of these words of John is that his consciousness was totally yielded to the Lord in communion with Him.

If we should have the idea right now that we want to be "in the Spirit" on any given day, I suggest that this is a matter of putting other things out of our minds, not thinking of anything else—and then thinking about the Lord Jesus Christ, letting the Holy Spirit show the things of Jesus Christ to us. If we were to devote ourselves in prayerful worship and think on the things that the Spirit brings to mind—Jesus Christ dying for us, Jesus Christ raised for us, Jesus Christ interceding on our behalf, Jesus Christ dwelling with us, Jesus Christ being in us—and then think those things through until by the working of the Holy Spirit, the presence of Jesus Christ would become more real in our consciousness than any other person or thing, we could well say that we were in the Spirit, namely, that the Spirit had control over our consciousness at that time.

THE VISION OF THE LIVING CHRIST
(Revelation 1:11-16)

"I was in the Spirit," namely, the Spirit completely controlling, overflowing, flooding me, "on the Lord's day." I understand this is the only time in the New Testament when the phrase "the Lord's day" is used.

Usually we speak of the first day of the week, and there is some question with some people as to what is meant by "the Lord's day." The consensus is that, from the usage in the early church, by "the Lord's day" we refer to "the first day of the week." Some people think this refers to the Sabbath Day, as if John were referring to the seventh day here. But the testimony of the early church as far as we have any evidence seems to be that it understood John to mean this happened to him on the Lord's day, namely Sunday.

John had been a great preacher. He had been pastor in the church of Ephesus. As much as we can gather from the history which is written about this time when John was a prisoner, taken away from his churches, Sunday was the day when those imprisoned pastors would be much in prayer for their distant congregations. "I was in the Spirit on the Lord's day, and heard behind me a great voice, as of a trumpet." It is hard for us to grasp all these things, but the words "voice, as of a trumpet" in Scripture always imply a message from heaven, as from God. John heard behind him a great voice, as of a trumpet, saying, "I am Alpha and Omega, the first and the last." This expression occurred in the eighth verse and is repeated here in verse 11.

> I am Alpha and Omega, the first and the last: and, What thou seest, write in a book, and send it unto the seven churches which are in Asia; unto Ephesus, and unto Smyrna, and unto Pergamos, and unto Thyatira, and unto Sardis, and unto Philadelphia, and unto Laodicea (1:11).

In the Scripture that follows, each one of these churches will be brought before us. To get used to the names of these churches, it is helpful to let them roll out of your mouth as you say them. Some of them you will recognize because we have names like them today. Some will be strange to you.

John was told what to do: "What thou seest, write in a book, and send it unto the seven churches which are in Asia."

> And I turned to see the voice that spake with me. And being turned, I saw seven golden candlesticks; and in the midst of the seven candlesticks one like unto the Son of man, clothed with a garment down to the foot, and girt about the paps with a golden girdle. His head and his hairs were white like wool, as white as snow; and his eyes were as a flame of fire; and his feet like unto fine brass, as if they burned in a furnace; and his voice as the sound of many waters. And he had in his right hand seven stars: and out of his mouth went a sharp two-edged sword: and his countenance was as the sun shineth in his strength (1:12-16).

Notice again the occurrence of the number "seven": seven churches, seven candlesticks, seven stars. The seven golden candlesticks bring to mind the seven-branched candlestick that was in the tabernacle and in the temple. The vision is not exactly the same, because John saw seven individual candlesticks, apparently set around as if in a circle. And in the midst of the seven, one like unto the Son of man. John then describes this person that was like the Son of man.

We recognize at once that his description is not like any picture of Jesus of Nazareth we ever saw hanging on a wall. There is something meaningful about that. The pictures of Jesus of Nazareth that we have seen are artists' conceptions of what Jesus of Nazareth may have looked like while He was here on earth. I do not want to be too critical in what I say about pictures of Jesus. But it is very characteristic that if the artist was a white man, he probably drew a picture of Jesus of Nazareth as a white man. If the artist was a Caucasian or a Northern European he would likely portray a Northern European. The fact of the matter is that Jesus of Nazareth was a Jew. He probably looked like a Jew and that is overlooked in most of the pictures we see, but it is not ultimately important. The reason for this is that nothing in the Bible encourages us to try to picture what Jesus of Nazareth looked like.

I defer to the good intentions of the artists and appreciate the spirit in which they drew the pictures. They drew the pictures because that was their way of passing on to us the nobility of the character they thought He had, and the lofty thoughts that they assumed would be shown on His face, as well as the compassion that they thought there would be in His countenance. That is what artists try to picture. Thus we have an artist's conception of what he thinks the character of Jesus of Nazareth would have looked like in human form. But there is not one single clue in Scripture about it. Not one. All we see in the pictures belongs to this world. That is of this earth. The only time I ever have any concern about that at all from an educational viewpoint is when I am disturbed that some people will get the idea that this is what the Lord Jesus Christ looks like now, because of course He does not.

As we consider John's vision, we may be sure that the Lord Jesus does not look like that now. The items in this vision are symbols. For instance, "Out of his mouth went a sharp two-edged sword." That would not go with any picture that we might have in our minds. If we have the New Testament Scriptures, we will remember that it speaks of the Word of God as being "sharper than a two-edged sword, piercing even to the dividing asunder of soul and spirit, and of the joints and marrow" (Heb. 4:12). That is the way the Bible speaks of itself. In the vision of the Lord Jesus Christ which John saw, out of His mouth went a sharp two-edged sword. He is the One who spoke the Word of God. So this seems right.

"His head and his hairs were white like wool, as white as snow." That is no inspiring picture. We do not think of that as a strong picture. But if we are acquainted with the Old Testament, as I am quite sure John's clientele was, and we knew what is written in the Book of Daniel, we would know that this is the way the Ancient of Days is pictured. In other words, when Daniel saw the vision of the Ancient of Days, of Almighty God, he saw Him with hair like that and with a head like that. Now, when John saw this one speaking to him, this one had the very appearance of the vision in Daniel. It seems obvious that John is being given to understand that this one speaking to him is the one whom Daniel saw, so the visions are related. It is that idea.

"His eyes were as a flame of fire." This is not exactly what we would ordinarily anticipate of those compassionate eyes we are expecting to meet. When we think of Christ Jesus looking down upon us with compassion, and we remember that He is touched with all the feelings of our infirmities, we do not particularly think of Him in our sorrow and grief as looking at us with eyes like "a flame of fire." But if we were going to be called to an account of our responsibility, if we were going to face the significance of our conduct, then to think of standing in the presence of the One who can see through us, before whom we are like an open book—that is pictured by John's penetrating vision of those eyes.

Then, "his feet like unto fine brass, as if they burned in a furnace; and his voice as the sound of many waters." Each of these aspects of Jesus' personality is linked with things in Scripture that have been associated with God and with eternity. What we have in this whole situation is that the living Lord Jesus Christ now has all the glory and the grandeur of Almighty God. He is really the Ruler of the heavens. And for the believers who lived as close to the earthly life of Jesus of Nazareth as those in the Asian churches did, it was a good thing for them to remember. The testimony of the Lord Jesus Christ while He was here on earth was that of a meek and humble person. When He was reviled, He reviled not again. When He was taken prisoner He did not fight. When the soldiers arrested Him and Peter wanted to fight for Him, He made Peter put away his sword. He said to Peter, "Thinkest thou that I cannot now pray to my Father, and he shall presently give me more than twelve legions of angels?" It was as if He had said, "They could not touch me if I just spoke the word." "But how then shall the scriptures be fulfilled, that thus it must be?" (Matt. 26:53-54).

What the world saw of Jesus of Nazareth was a humble, meek, inoffensive, harmless person who came to give Himself a ransom for sinners. And that is wonderfully true, but that is not the whole truth. You and I could be left with what might properly be considered a rather touching and a rather sweet impression of the Lord Jesus Christ. But this would be quite inadequate if we did not know more than that. Right here, at the beginning of the Book of Revelation, we are to understand that there is One standing in the midst of the churches, with the seven churches around Him, carrying on His head as it were the glory of God, gird about ready for service, with golden girdle. This One who holds in His hand seven stars (and we will consider later what these are). The One from whose mouth goes a two-edged sword. The One whose voice sounds like the rushing of many waters.

Every one of these aspects goes beyond this world. There is not a thing like this on earth. Our Lord Jesus Christ in His present glory is almighty, great, high, holy. He is Lord. And He is walking in the midst of the churches with eyes that penetrate, with a mouth that speaks the truth. That is who this One is: our Lord Jesus Christ.

Chapter 2

CHRIST IN THE MIDST OF THE CHURCHES
(Revelation 1:17–2:5)

> And when I saw him, I fell at his feet as dead. And he laid his
> right hand upon me, saying unto me, Fear not; I am the first and
> the last: I am he that liveth, and was dead; and, behold, I am
> alive for evermore, Amen; and have the keys of hell and of death
> (1:17-18).

We should note the very words that the Lord Jesus speaks
here. Because John fell at His feet as one dead, Jesus said,
"Fear not; I am the first and the last." That had been said
before. No less than three times this statement occurs in this
script, "I am the eternal God." Clearly this emphasizes that
this same person—Jesus of Nazareth as He was on earth,
Jesus Christ as He is now—is the eternal God.

"I am he that liveth, and was dead": He was the Resurrected One. "Behold, I am alive for evermore": He is the
Eternal One. "Amen" means "so let it be," as if John couldn't
help but say that. "And have the keys of hell and death": if
Christ has the keys of hell and death it means to bring to our
mind that this Almighty God, this Almighty Lord, our Savior
has in His hands the power to overcome hell and death.

> Write the things which thou hast seen, and the things which
> are, and the things which shall be hereafter (1:19).

I am not sure that this saying means three separate kinds of
things. I am not sure that certain things are the ones that John
saw, that different things are the ones "which are," that other
things are the ones "which shall be hereafter." I am inclined

to think that, in the single vision John had, these are three different ways of saying what he thought. "The things which thou hast seen": these are the very things which are and these are the very things which shall be. They not only were at the time John saw them on the isle of Patmos, but they will be that way forever. Now, I know other use is made of those words, but this is the thought that comes to me.

> The mystery of the seven stars which thou sawest in my right hand, and the seven golden candlesticks . . . (1:20).

The word "mystery" refers to hidden truth. "Mystery" is something we cannot see on the surface. It refers to the real inward meaning. Now the Lord gives to John the real meaning of the seven stars.

> . . . The seven stars are the angels of the seven churches: and the seven candlesticks which thou sawest are the seven churches (1:20).

I will have something to point out about "the angels of the churches" in chapters 2 and 3 of this Book of Revelation. But just now, for our purpose here, let us consider the seven stars.

In verse 16 it is written that Jesus had in His right hand seven stars. Here in verse 20 He states clearly that these seven stars are "the angels" of the seven churches, the representatives of the seven churches. From this we understand that He is the One who holds the churches in His hand. We remember that Jesus said, "My Father, which gave them me, is greater than all; and no man is able to pluck them out of my Father's hand" (John 10:29). So let us be confident, since this Almighty Being holds the whole church in His hand.

The seven candlesticks are the seven churches. Christ the Lord is the One who moves in the midst of the churches. He is moving right now amid the churches. Let us note these two things in this first chapter about this Almighty Being as John saw the vision: Christ the Lord holds the churches in His hand, and He will never let them go. And He walks in the midst of the churches.

We shall see in Revelation 2 and 3 how His eyes penetrate. He is the living Lord. He has not turned His back on the churches; He is in the very midst of the churches. He sees, knows, understands everything that is going on in the churches; He is not going to let anything slip. He is holding the churches, but He sees them.

While we think of this with reference to the churches, let every believer think of it with reference to himself. Each believer should remember that he personally is in a very real sense the church as far as the Lord Jesus Christ is concerned. The Lord deals with each believer. Many of the things said about the church are said about the individual believer. The church is a temple of the Holy Spirit: the individual believer is a temple of the Holy Spirit. The church is the body of Christ: believers are the members of the body of Christ. Christ is in the church: Christ is in the believer, the hope of glory. So when we think about this Scripture, we can have this particular thought with us in a special way. This living Almighty Being holds believers like those stars in His hands. He will never let them go. And this Almighty Being lives, is in our midst, sees us, knows us.

> Unto the angel of the church of Ephesus write; These things saith he that holdeth the seven stars in his right hand, who walketh in the midst of the seven golden candlesticks (2:1).

Here is that same idea again—those two aspects: Christ holds the church, and Christ judges the church. He sees the church. We can have in mind that when we say Christ judges the churches, He is not judging as if He wants to get rid of them. He is judging them as One who will cleanse them. This living Lord whom John saw in the vision is actually involved in the life of His people, the church.

> I know thy works, and thy labour, and thy patience, and how thou canst not bear them which are evil: and thou hast tried them which say they are apostles, and are not, and hast found them liars: and hast borne, and hast patience, and for my name's sake hast laboured, and hast not fainted. Nevertheless I have somewhat against thee, because thou hast left thy first love (2:2-4).

We cannot help but ask ourselves, is it possible that a person could work, labor, have patience and be true and be careful, and bear things, and do things, hold on with things, and be steadfast; and yet leave his first love? Yes. Read this:

> Remember therefore from whence thou art fallen, and repent, and do the first works . . . (2:5).

It is sometimes a chilling thing to hear some of us in the ministry. Sometimes you can listen to one of us preachers and you miss the note of warm, fervent love and affection to the Lord Jesus Christ. There are times it is not clear the preacher loves the Lord. That is not good. The Lord notices that.

"Do the first works." The people were to act as they did in the beginning. One time years ago I heard this criticism of me and the ministry, that I was acting the way I had in the beginning. I prayed then and I pray now that it may still be true of me. But I was criticized for this in Dallas, Texas, when a farmer friend of mine came down from another part of the country and visited in that area and met one of the other ministers. The other minister told my friend, "Yes, he maintains the enthusiasm of a new convert." It was said disparagingly. When I heard it, I humbly asked the Lord, "Oh God, keep me that way." I would love to live all my life with the enthusiasm of a new convert. If I could, I would. That is my prayer.

"Do the first works." When we get to where a question arises as to whether we ever did love the Lord, we must bring it back: what did we do when we first loved the Lord? We should do it again. Do it just like that. He will notice it. He notices the first works.

As Revelation 2 opens, John's vision is of the living Lord Jesus Christ standing in the midst of the churches. Seven churches are named. I have already intimated that I am inclined to think the seven churches refer to the whole church on earth: seven being the number of completeness, thus referring to the whole church. These seven individual churches actually existed in Asia Minor just as they are named. But the facts seem plain that there were many more churches than seven in that region. These seven may not have been distinctly the biggest or the strongest or the worst churches.

It is quite likely that each one of these churches had exactly the characteristics named here in chapters 2 and 3. But the idea which I think is intended is not that these churches were peculiar, but that what the church at Ephesus had, other churches will have; what the church at Smyrna had, other churches will have; and what the church at Pergamos had, other churches will have; and so on. In other words, if we take the seven characteristics seen in these seven churches, we can get some idea of what the Lord Jesus Christ, the Head of the Church, sees now in His people on earth. He sees the good and the bad. He is standing in the midst of us as our Judge.

The great truth John will bring to all who read his letter is that the Lord stands in the midst of His church and sees everything. It is wonderful to note in each instance that, although He sees the whole truth, Christ keeps an open door for their blessing. There is not one of the churches to whom He does not promise rich blessing. He sees them spiritually as they are: in six of the seven instances He gives a definite rebuke. In each case He draws attention to a failing that could hurt them badly. Each blemish is serious enough to hurt the church so badly that its candlestick would be moved out of place.

The single church for which no blemish is noted is the second named, the church of Smyrna. This church apparently was facing grave danger from the outside. It was a church facing persecution. But with all He saw, Jesus Christ knew that blessing was possible even in blemished churches.

"THOU HAST LEFT THY FIRST LOVE"
(Revelation 2:2-5)

When we look at the church at Ephesus in Revelation 2, we see that the Lord points out first what He knows about their works. He names nine good things.

> I know thy works, and thy labour, and thy patience, and how thou canst not bear them which are evil . . . (2:2).

It is enough to make us pause and wonder if we are inclined to become too easygoing with ourselves or with other people, spiritually speaking. The Lord takes note of the sensitiveness of the heart which is not able to endure what is evil in the sight of God.

> . . . And thou hast tried them which say they are apostles, and are not, and hast found them liars (2:2).

There were some coming into the church at Ephesus who claimed to be ministers of the gospel, but they were not. The church at Ephesus had the strength to find out that they were not and to expose them as impostors.

The Book of Acts records that occasion when the apostle Paul gathered the elders of Ephesus together and warned them.

> For I know this, that after my departing shall grievous wolves enter in among you, not sparing the flock (Acts 20:29).

Paul warned the elders to watch for those who pretended to preach the gospel but did not preach really from their heart. Here in Revelation, the Lord Jesus is saying to them that they had tried persons who claimed to be apostles, and they found them to be liars.

> And hast borne, and hast patience, and for my name's sake hast laboured, and hast not fainted (2:3).

The church at Ephesus had been a strong church that had endured throughout all that generation. John is generally considered to have been the pastor of that church and if so, he was probably pastor for a considerable length of time. But when he wrote about these things, he was reporting what the Lord Jesus said about the church to him.

> Nevertheless I have somewhat against thee, because thou hast left thy first love (2:4).

It seems to be possible for a person to be a strong, intelligent, committed, active, faithful, patient believer in Christ, and yet have this trait which holds such dire dangers deep down in his heart because he has left his first love of the Lord Jesus Christ. Here again is the evidence that the living Lord Jesus looks on the heart. The first thing He wants is a right personal relationship with Him, personal faithfulness to Himself. Nothing will take its place. No zeal for a doctrine, no endurance of persecution in a controversy, no faithfulness in a crisis, no sacrifice in a church program, no contribution to any church or missionary work or for the poor will ever compensate. There is no good thing a believer can do to take the place of his personal face-to-face relationship with Jesus Christ. The apostle Paul told the Corinthians:

> If any man love not the Lord Jesus Christ, let him be Anathema Maranatha [accursed] (1 Cor. 16:22).

Paul also said to the Corinthians:

> Though I speak with the tongues of men and of angels, and have not charity, I am become as sounding brass, or a tinkling cymbal. And though I have the gift of prophecy, and understand all mysteries, and all knowledge; and though I have all faith, so that I could remove mountains, and have not charity, I am nothing. And though I bestow all my goods to feed the poor, and though I give my body to be burned, and have not charity, it profiteth me nothing (1 Cor. 13:1-3).

That is the way Paul put it.

In this matter of loving the Lord, your heart could say with mine, "How can I do it?" The truth is that no man can do it in himself. On one occasion when I was the pastor of a church, I was afflicted beyond words with a deep sense of dismay, frustration, and despair when I realized deep down in me that my heart was not warm toward the Lord Jesus Christ. And I was afraid of what the Scriptures said. They spoke to me and I condemned myself out of hand, but what bothered me was, I did not know what to do. I was a minister, the pastor of a church. But how could I love the Lord? I did not find in me what was needed to worship God.

Then I remembered that the same feeling had come to me earlier in my life, and I remembered also that I never would have what I needed in my heart of clay. No human being has it in him to worship God. The natural heart is enmity against the law of God. It is not subject to the law of God, nor can it be. One may well ask, "Then what can I do?" It finally came to me at three o'clock in the morning, on the lawn behind our manse where I was out under the stars, crying out to God in my soul for something that would fit me to preach. I hated to go into the pulpit as a liar. I believed the gospel, I believed in God, but my own conscience bore me witness that I did not love Him as I wanted to love Him, as He is worthy to be loved, with the fervor that there should be. I just did not have it. And when I tried to get it, I couldn't. No matter what I did, there was nothing in my heart, and I was shocked. I began to wonder whether I was even a believer in Christ.

Then in that night, in that early morning hour, as I looked up into a starlit sky, it came to me so clearly: this human heart of mine is merely clay. It is like the earth in the nearby flower bed. Suddenly I realized enough to know that the earth in that flower bed left to itself would never produce flowers. As a matter of fact, left to itself it would be so cold as to freeze. Do you know what is needed? The sun must shine. It is the shining of the sun that makes the ground warm enough to germinate the seeds and cause the flowers to grow. This soil has no heat of its own that is adequate. It is the sun's shining upon it that makes this earth warm enough to produce living conditions. Then I knew about this heart of mine: cold, naturally earth, dust of the dust. We are just made of the earth. But when the sun in the face of the Lord Jesus Christ shines into these cold hearts of ours, it warms them. "We love Him because He first loved us."

The thing to do when one feels cold is to move the flower pot into the sunlight. Let the sun shine on it. We should take that heart of ours to the cross of Calvary, look up again into the blessed face of the One who died for us, and then by ourselves, individually and alone, take it all to ourselves and believe it to be true. We will find we can no more help believing Him than we could help getting warm if we walked out in the hot sun. Anytime we go out into the hot sun we will get warm. And anytime we will open our hearts to what the Lord Jesus did for us on Calvary's cross, we will get warm. Do you want to love Him? Then look at His love for you.

And this is how to do the first works. That is what He told the Ephesians to do. "Remember therefore from whence thou art fallen." We believing people should call back to mind how it was with us when we first became believers. Perchance sometime after we became a believer in Christ, we had some high mountaintop experience, some occasion when we drew nigh unto God. We should remember that and not give ourselves credit for what it was, but just thank the Lord for the way it was. He lifted us to that point.

"Remember therefore from whence thou art fallen, and repent." Repentance is not a matter of feeling sorry. "Godly sorrow worketh repentance." Sorrow is all right: it has its proper place. If we have been doing something we should not have done, or if we have left undone something that we ought to have done, feeling sorrow on our part is quite right. But that is not repentance. Repentance is a judgment of oneself. When we feel the sorrow in our heart, we should turn it in on ourselves and say about ourselves what Isaiah the prophet said of himself, "I am undone; because I am a man of unclean lips, and I dwell in the midst of a people of unclean lips" (Isa. 6:5). If we want to repent, we simply say to ourselves, "I am cold. The Lord died for me, and I forgot this. He gave Himself for me, and I have done nothing for Him." We should see it, think it, and judge ourselves, and then ask the Lord to forgive us. He will. "If we confess our sins, he is faithful and just to forgive us our sins, and to cleanse us from all unrighteousness" (1 John 1:9).

The only big thing the matter with us is sin. And where sin abounds, grace does much more abound. So when we repent, we come into the presence of God, we acknowledge our own shortcomings as we see them and feel them. If we look into His face and let Him work on us, we do "the first works." We do the first thing that comes to us: if He gave everything for us, we cannot help but want to give everything to Him. When He reaches a hand down to us, we feel like taking His hand. That is doing the first works. This is doing what we did when we first turned to the Lord. Doing what we did when we first realized what He had done for us. Why did we do it then? Because it was the obvious thing. And it will be that way again.

> Remember therefore from whence thou art fallen, and repent, and do the first works; or else I will come unto thee quickly, and will remove thy candlestick out of his place, except thou repent (2:5).

I am not sure that I can do the full justice in interpreting this. Somehow I do not think that this is so much a warning that the rebuked church is to be destroyed forever, as that their testimony, their place of testimony, will be taken away. The candlestick seems to represent the light that the church shows to the whole world. This seems to be a warning to that church that if it does not recall to itself those early first-love experiences, and does not quicken within its heart that first love for the Lord Jesus Christ that He wants, He will remove the candlestick of that church out of its place. Apparently the testimony of that church will be blacked out unless it repents.

THE DEEDS OF THE NICOLAITANS
(Revelation 2:6-7)

> But this thou hast, that thou hatest the deeds of the Nicolaitans, which I also hate (2:6).

This verse is another one of those places where our limitations become obvious. Not only for myself, but in every place that I have read, I know of no one who has been able to say in a completely satisfying way what this means.

The word "Nicolaitans" is simply an English transliteration of the Greek word. What that Greek word means no one knows. We assume—and this seems to be the general opinion—that the root of the word is in the word "laity," and that the meaning is what we have in mind when we speak of the clergy and the laity of the church. There seems to be a strong inclination to think that the "Nicolaitans" were people who had a way of separating the church into clergy and laity. Thus there were some who thought the clergy were a special class and the laity were another class.

If this is so, then this verse indicates that the Lord disapproves of that separation. Of all the different scholars I have read, more than 50 percent are disposed to think of the verse that way. But I want to admit as a matter of fact that it seems no one knows for certain. Yet, whoever these Nicolaitans were, they seem to have been a party of a particular sort in the church at Ephesus, and for some reason the Lord Jesus hated their deeds. What we can know for certain is that the church hated them too; and the Lord was pleased about that.

Let us take note of this truth. In the church at Ephesus there was a group of people who had a particular point of view which offended the Lord. That their characteristic is obscure to us I trust to the providence of God; I am satisfied it is obscure because it does not make any difference whether we know it clearly. But there is a great and clear truth here to keep in mind: in the church there can be practices which the Lord does not want. And He takes note whether a congregation tolerates such things. He hates such things. I don't like to use the word "hate," but I must. It is obvious that the Lord Jesus looking down on His believing followers may see certain traits that He hates. And He notes when the congregation as a whole hates the things that He hates. And I think that is a shoe that can fit on any foot, whoever we happen to be, whatever church we are in.

This Scripture tells me that whenever I am in any group of believing people, whenever I am in any church, in any denominational meeting with any company of people, any kind of gathering at all, there is one thing I should be sensitive about: What is in this meeting with which my Lord in heaven would be pleased? That I am to endorse. What is there in this meeting with which my Lord in heaven would be displeased? That I am to hate. This will involve sober reflection, because sometimes we can be together with believing people and find them doing things that do not seem to be like what the Lord Jesus would do. We know He is the same yesterday, today, and forever. And what He wants of us is that we are to love what He loves, and we are to hate what He hates. This church in Ephesus had that quality, and He appreciated it.

> He that hath an ear, let him hear what the Spirit saith unto the churches; To him that overcometh will I give to eat of the tree of life, which is in the midst of the paradise of God (2:7).

The special difficulty in this particular church was a coldness of heart. With all the achievements of these saints, this blemish affected them all. To the person who would overcome that, to the person who would be victorious in his relationship to the Lord, He would give to eat of the tree of life.

As we read on in Revelation we may notice that each message to one of the seven churches shows one of the identifying marks of the vision which describes the Lord Jesus Christ in chapter 1. When we then take the promises He makes with reference to each of these churches—"to him that overcometh"—we have an amazing compendium of the promises of the Lord Jesus Christ to the church as a whole.

THE MEANING OF NUMBERS

At this point I want to discuss the use of numbers in the Book of Revelation. I present this very humbly and very tentatively, having this in mind, that nowhere in the Bible will we find word for word what I am going to say here. What I say is, I believe, the consensus of Bible students as I have been able to discern it, and it seems credible.

This leads me to say something about our understanding of the Bible. The Bible seems to be so written and so presented that, in the last analysis, only the Holy Spirit of God can give us the truth we should have; we should get the really new ideas from the face of the Lord Jesus Christ, who loved us and gave Himself for us. I think God has reserved to Himself the right to open the eyes of our understanding as we see the truth in the face of the Lord Jesus Christ. Apart from our personally depending on the Lord Jesus for our salvation, words are to no avail to tell us the meaning of the gospel.

The number *one* in the Bible ordinarily simply suggests unity. It is not one in a series like 1, 2, 3, 4, 5, or like 1 out of 2 or 3 or 4 or 5, but it is one in the sense of altogether in one. This is the usual meaning, but the number is not used that way symbolically in the Book of Revelation. Husband and wife are to become one; "I and my Father are one"; "that they all may be one as we are one" is the prayer of the Lord in chapter 17 of John's Gospel: in all these, one refers to unity.

The number *two* is used several times in the Book of Revelation. Two suggests added strength, added weight, increased strength, or multiplied courage. It is a common feeling among human beings that two people together on a subject are stronger than two single people at some distance from each other. "If two of you shall agree on earth as touching any thing that they shall ask" (Matt. 18:19). When the Lord Jesus sent out His disciples, the seventy, He sent them out two by two (Luke 10:1). We are going to read about two witnesses who will be preaching in the city of Jerusalem. When we read later about seeing beasts in the vision, there are two. Generally speaking, this leaves you with the impression that whatever is implied there is doubled; that means added strength. The idea seems to be suggested by the fact that there are two instead of just one.

Three is considered in Scripture—and commonly among people both far and wide—to refer to deity or to God. Of course, for us who are believers in Christ we see in that the Trinity. The general impression of three seems to be to convey the idea of adequacy. Three sides, the three sides of the triangle, imply sufficiency. Wherever there are three, we have something that is adequate and competent, but chiefly with the idea of God. We have three woes: evidently that is just as many woes as we can endure. Three plagues, which could be just as many plagues as we can endure. Three gates on each side of the walls of Jerusalem, which means just as many openings as we will need. In other words, God is all we will ever need when we have three. That is the general impression people gain, but particularly referring to God, as we shall see.

Now, *four* seems to be generally used about things that refer to the earth. There are various reasons for this. Take, for instance, the common expression "the four corners of the earth"—and also the four directions, north, south, east, and west. If we think of the four points of the compass, we have "the four corners of the earth." Then there are the four winds of the earth, when the wind blows from the north or the south or the east or the west. There are no other winds, are there? There is just about all the wind possible, and that would cover the earth.

Now, things are like that wherever we have four. It is suggested that when we find the four living creatures in the Book of Revelation, we could well think of all nature. Those living creatures seem to refer to natural things. That will be for all the earthly creatures, all nature. Four angels at four corners controlling the four winds from heaven seem to imply heavenly control over what goes on on earth. The four horsemen go forth into the history of the world. The four angels are bound at the Euphrates River, and so on. But four seems to refer to the earth in the biblical usage.

Most people know that seven is generally considered to be the number of perfection. This is interesting, because seven is made up of four and three. If we took the whole of the earth and the whole of heaven and put them together we would get seven. Four of earth and three of God put together make seven. Seven seems to be the combination of heaven and the earth put together to give completeness or perfection. The number seven occurs fifty-four times in the Book of Revelation. This suggests that what John was seeing in the revelation in a certain sense was the ultimate, the complete thing.

To speak of the seven spirits of God, as in Revelation 1:4, there is great difficulty with the symbolism of seven if we count the number seven as being 1-2-3-4-5-6-7. The Scriptures commonly speak of the Holy Spirit, one Spirit. But if we think of the sevenfold Spirit of God, or the complete Spirit of God, or the total Spirit of God, or the perfect Spirit of God, then the seven commends itself much more readily.

It might be well to note that there are two other numbers related to seven in the Book of Revelation. A broken seven— completeness or perfection broken—is three and one-half. Three and one-half occurs a number of times in the Book of Revelation and always with something troublesome. It is perfection broken. That seems to imply something is incomplete, imperfect, indefinite. In some places it is written as forty-two months, which is three and one-half years. In Revelation 11:3 there is written "a thousand two hundred and threescore days"— or 1,260—and we might say "Oh my, that is another number." But when we allow thirty days to the month, then the forty-two months makes 1,260 days. And that is again three and one-half years. Three and one-half years always brings the idea of something incomplete or imperfect or indefinite. It is a broken seven, broken perfection.

Let us consider the number six. It is interesting that wherever the number six is used, it always has an evil connotation. If we take seven as the ideal, of the perfect thing, what is six? Six is something that falls just short of perfection, just did not make it. It is something not right. That is six. When we think about the words and the terms that have to do with the evil that will be mentioned, six is used, as we will see. When John undertakes to indicate man at his very worst, he says the number of man is 666. This number is the worst we could say. That seems to be implied in its use in Revelation.

Some of you may by chance say here, as I am writing along,

"That is just too intricate or too fantastic for me." I can tell you that for more than twenty years of my life after I became a believer I thought the same way. The only reason I present this now is that we are going to be beset with numbers in the Book of Revelation. They will be all around us as we read, and I am offering you a way of sensing their significance. In case some of you are hearing this for the first time, let me suggest to you that even among us today many people have the feeling that the number thirteen is unlucky.

Let us go on to consider the number ten. It seems that ten is associated with the idea of secular completeness: earthly, worldly completeness. A man has ten fingers and ten toes if he is a normal man. The word ten also implies totality as far as this world is concerned. The Ten Commandments are the total Word of God with reference to man's earthly activity.

Now, if we take seven, the number for completeness and perfectness, and ten, which is total adequacy, and multiply them—seven times ten—we get seventy. With the Jewish people, the word seventy meant all there was. Seventy times anything means all there is. The apostle Peter asked Jesus of Nazareth whether or not he ought to forgive his brother seven times. He was told, "I say not unto thee, Until seven times: but, Until seventy times seven" (Matt. 18:21). I do not think anyone seriously thinks that Peter was supposed to count occasions of forgiveness up to 490 and then quit. Seventy times seven meant on and on for all time. Since seven means completeness, when he asked, "Shall I forgive him seven times?" he had in mind total, complete forgiveness—perfection. He was told, "No, seventy times seven," which means on and on and on to always: that, Jesus implied, would be perfect.

The number twelve seems to be associated with God's people on earth. I offer this to you very tentatively: God's people on earth. Twelve is made up of three times four. If three is God Divine and four is earth, then when God gets into the earth, as He does with His people, it is twelve. There were twelve tribes. We speak of the twelve patriarchs, the heads of those tribes. There were twelve apostles. And in the Book of Revelation there are twelve and twelve, twenty-four elders around the throne. It fits very well if there are twenty-four elders around the throne: we could simply say that God's people in both Old and New Testament times are represented: the twelve patriarchs in the Old Testament and the twelve apostles in the New Testament, grouping together. Other twelves come to mind. For example, each of the tribes had twelve thousand members in the list in Revelation 7.

The number thousand is derived from ten that implies secular completeness: a thousand is ten times ten times ten—that is, ten cubed. This suggests simply a symbolic amount of unknown quantity or length. And the thousand at any time means, as far as this world is concerned, all of it. God's people are identified as being twelve thousand. This may sound fantastic to some of you, but let me go on with it and point out that God's people would be God's three times earth's four to make twelve thousand. All of God's people in the tribes could be implied by the twelve thousand. And of course, twelve times twelve thousand makes 144,000. So the 144,000 saints whom John saw would merely be representative of all the people of God, of all time, when we are using these numbers in this symbolic fashion.

Let us think about the thousand years referred to in Revelation 20. That is the only place in the Book of Revelation that the thousand-year period is mentioned. It is mentioned six times in that one chapter. But that is the only chapter in which it is mentioned. It is possible that for the thousand years, there could be in mind an indefinite length of time, an unnumbered amount of time. Let us not forget the words of 2 Peter 3:8: "One day is with the Lord as a thousand years, and a thousand years as one day." This truth is just to keep anyone from trying to use a calendar. We should not use a calendar with God.

When these words and ideas come up in the Book of Revelation, we will take note of them. When we think of twelve as being God and the earth together—three times four—and we think of the twelve apostles, and God's working in them here on earth, that makes sense. That fits. Why not use it? It will not hurt us. And we have something there that is suggestive to us, to help us to remember the symbolism.

SMYRNA
(Revelation 2:8-11)

Of the seven churches listed in Revelation 2 and 3, Smyrna and Philadelphia are the only two of whom no criticism is recorded.

> And unto the angel of the church in Smyrna write; These things saith the first and the last, which was dead, and is alive; I know thy works, and tribulation, and poverty, (but thou art rich) and I know the blasphemy of them which say they are Jews, and are not, but are the synagogue of Satan. Fear none of those things which thou shalt suffer: behold, the devil shall cast some of you into prison, that ye may be tried; and ye shall have tribulation ten days: be thou faithful unto death, and I will give thee a crown of life. He that hath an ear, let him hear what the Spirit saith unto the churches; He that overcometh shall not be hurt of the second death (2:8-11).

This was a short, almost sweet, comforting word of assurance to a congregation facing bitter and deadly persecution. It reminds one of Paul's letter to the Philippians. The Philippians as a young church were facing persecution. Paul was in prison at the time, in danger of death, yet Philippians is one epistle in which there is no breath of criticism about the church. Rather, there is an undertone of strong joy in the face of death. Writing to that church, the apostle Paul says, "For me to live is Christ, and to die is gain." That is the way he wrote to people who were about to face death.

There is something we need to keep in mind about the testimony of believers in the world. There are people today in jail because they believe. There are people today who are without shelter because they believe. There are people being beaten today because they believe in the Lord Jesus Christ. There are people who are being bitterly persecuted, and some have seen their loved ones die, because they believe in the Lord Jesus Christ. We see that is all involved in being a believer in Christ.

Being a believer involves much more than just what I happen to go through at any one time. We all belong to that church which at this or that or the other place is right now suffering. When we think of these seven churches—Ephesus for one, Smyrna for this one, then Pergamos, then Thyatira, and then Sardis, then Philadelphia, then Laodicea—we note that they do not all have the same experience. These seven churches all existed in Asia Minor in the same region, but the congregations did not share the same experiences.

This church at Smyrna was facing and enduring bitter tribulation. The thing for us to understand is that the gospel of Christ shines bright and clear for the woman who is going to die because she believes; and for the man who will be killed because he believes; and for the mother who will see her son taken out to be shot because he believes. Faith in Christ, the gospel of Christ, is to her and to that son a sense of holy triumph in this situation—because even when he is shot, he has not lost a thing that really matters. He belongs to the Lord, and the moment he is killed here, he goes right into the very presence of almighty God. And so when we find a church here that is facing dire persecution and might even be wiped out, there may be no lament. There is no hanging of the crepe on the door. There is no long-faced sense of defeat. There is a sturdy, steady, lisping joy that they are victors over death. If it should happen that they die, there would be a quick trip to the presence of God. After all, they are going to live forever.

If some of us are going to stay down here and live out our threescore years and ten in a situation in which we are beset on every side with temptations of ease and comfort, we have in some sense spiritually a much harder row to hoe. It is a hard thing for us to maintain ourselves close to the Lord when every day we are given opportunity to sit down in ease and peace as far as this world is concerned. Let us be very careful that we do not equate the blessing of God with something I can enjoy tomorrow. Let us have in mind that the blessing of God is in terms of personal fellowship with Him now. If it pleased Him that we should live, and if it pleased Him that we should have health, and if it would please Him that we should have peace, we shall be able to thank Him. And we pray that in this prosperity our hearts will not be weak.

The church in Smyrna was facing trouble. "I know thy works, and tribulation." That is the first fact. They had real trouble and poverty. Their goods had been confiscated. They lost their property. They were made poor because they believed. But the Lord puts in this word, "but thou art rich." He then adds, "And I know the blasphemy of them which say

they are Jews, and are not, but are the synagogue of Satan."
Among the Smyrna Christians there were people who claimed
to be believers but were not. The writer here I think implies
that just because a person was a Jew physically did not mean
that he was a Jew spiritually. And these people who said they
were Jews because they were born of Jews—and are not because they do not believe like Abraham, "but are the
synagogue of Satan"—are the ones to whom He refers. He
may very well be referring to persecution which was incited
and led by members of the Jewish faith at that time, in that
place.

"Fear none of those things which thou shalt suffer." They
were going to suffer. I think I am among those people that are
so ready to think that the blessing of God means that everything will be victory and sunshine, assuming victory to be
good fortune. But note this:

> And what shall I more say? for the time would fail me to tell of
> Gideon, and of Barak, and of Samson, and of Jephthah; of
> David also, and Samuel, and of the prophets: Who through
> faith subdued kingdoms, wrought righteousness, obtained
> promises, stopped the mouths of lions, quenched the violence
> of fire, escaped the edge of the sword, out of weakness were
> made strong, waxed valiant in fight, turned to flight the armies
> of the aliens. Women received their dead raised to life again:
> and others were tortured, not accepting deliverance; that they
> might obtain a better resurrection (Heb. 11:32-35).

This is one unending description of victory after victory after
victory over circumstances. But note in the middle of this
passage the words "And others were tortured." Never think
that torture shows any lack of faith, never think that being
tortured means God has forgotten you. "Not accepting deliverance," they would not let themselves be taken out of the
danger they were in. To what purpose? "That they might
obtain a better resurrection."

Never think that when someone gets hurt it means he was
out of the will of God. You and I as believers in Christ should
get hold of that truth. Here is a church that would be blotted
out, whose members would be killed. This is not defeat, nor
God forsaking them; this is a glowing, burning tribute to the
glory of God of people willing to die in the Lord Jesus Christ
that they might obtain a better resurrection. "Fear none of

those things which thou shalt suffer."

"Ye shall have tribulation ten days." This is one place where I think the figure ten is a symbolic number. I do not think it means ten days by the calendar as from the eleventh to the twenty-first of the month. These ten days, I believe, are using the word ten to mean secular completeness. "Be thou faithful unto death." It does not say, "Be thou faithful until you win out on this earth" nor "Be thou faithful until in providence you suddenly get wealthy." No. "Be thou faithful unto death" because you are going to die.

"And I will give thee a crown of life. He that hath an ear, let him hear what the Spirit saith unto the churches; He that overcometh shall not be hurt of the second death." These seven churches, as we read of them, actually give us seven different aspects of the experience of a believer in Christ. There will be a flavor of this in the life of any one of us. It will come out more or less. There are people this very day whose experience will be like those in this church at Smyrna. It may be spiritual persecution rather than physical. But there have been people in Uganda and elsewhere in the world who have experienced it physically in this fashion.

PERGAMOS
(Revelation 2:12-14)

> And to the angel of the church in Pergamos write; These things saith he which hath the sharp sword with two edges (2:12).

We all have in mind that the two-edged sword refers to Scripture and recalls the vision of Jesus Christ in the first chapter of Revelation. Jesus is the one who speaks the Word of God.

"I know thy works." As we read through chapters 2 and 3 we notice that to each church the Lord says, "I know thy works." When He says this, He means more than just "I have heard of your works." He means that He knows they have been active. This is "know" in the sense of "appraise." He understands their conduct. He appreciates and knows everything they have done. He has evaluated and judged everything that they have done. "I know thy works."

> I know thy works, and where thou dwellest, even where Sa-
> tan's seat is (2:13).

I remember that I was a believer in Christ for some length of
time before I read this passage slowly, and this word gave me
quite a shock. Here was a church, a congregation, that resided
where Satan's seat is! It is good for us always to keep in mind
that Satan is not now in the lake of fire. If he were there we
would be much better off. As a matter of fact, Peter wrote that
Satan goes about as a roaring lion, seeking whom he may
devour (1 Peter 5:8). But this is probably symbolic language,
because he does not roar enough to scare us: he is far too
smooth for that. He is the smooth, subtle, cunning enemy of
our souls. But here in Pergamos, he had a seat in the church.
That is what this verse means. Look at it.

> I know thy works, and where thou dwellest, even where
> Satan's seat is: and thou holdest fast my name, and hast
> not denied my faith, even in those days wherein Antipas was
> my faithful martyr, who was slain among you, where Satan
> dwelleth (2:13).

How would you know Satan? Well, there is one thing about
the popular idea of Satan that has been no help to believing
people, especially to young believers. It is the poetic conception of him having horns and tail and big hoofs. Of course,
when one does not see any such creature running around, it is
natural to think the devil is not around—which is a big mistake. On one occasion when Satan tempted the Lord Jesus
Christ it was through Peter, Jesus' own apostle. If Peter had
realized he was being used he would have choked. He never
intended for his conduct to tempt His master. Peter really
thought he was showing his devotion to the Lord when he said
to Him, "Don't go to Jerusalem. Don't let them kill you. Let
this thing be far from thee." We remember that the Lord
turned to him and said, "Get thee behind me, Satan" (Matt.
16:23). That was a close friend. Satan does not have a body; he
is a spirit.

We know several things about Satan. When Michael the
archangel strove with Satan over the body of Moses, he dared
not rail at him but could only say, "The Lord rebuke thee." In
that light it would be foolish to say anything careless about
Satan. I will just repeat like a child something of what the

Scriptures say about Satan. For one thing he is a liar. As a liar he is smooth. Would you know about a smooth liar? He never looks like one.

The second thing I know about Satan is that he is the accuser of the brethren. Any time we are inclined to find fault with other people, we need to be very careful. We do not find in scriptural record one time when the Lord Jesus uncovered the private sins of one person to anybody else. Not one time. He spoke straight to the woman at the well: "Thou hast well said thou hast no husband. Thou hast had five husbands. And the one thou livest with now is not thy husband" (John 4). But that was to her. Jesus did speak of a group of people, the Pharisees. And He privately dealt with people. But He did not expose private sins to others. We should think of that. If we were to fall into the temptation of bringing out in public things that could hurt other people, we would not be like our Lord. We would be like the devil: He is the accuser of the brethren. He is a murderer. He means to do harm.

> But I have a few things against thee, because thou hast there them that hold the doctrine of Balaam, who taught Balak to cast a stumblingblock before the children of Israel, to eat things sacrificed unto idols, and to commit fornication (2:14).

This passage refers to an Old Testament incident. The doctrine of Balaam is a compromise with the enemies of God. It means getting along with ungodly people, joining in with unbelievers. Sometimes the suggestion comes that maybe we could join in and help them. Evil presents for us a one-way street. What I mean by that can be illustrated this way. Suppose a woman were going to bake a cake that needed six eggs. If she had five good eggs and one bad one, and she mixed them, the batter would be all bad. You say, "That is not fair." I know, but the thing to do is not to use any bad eggs. Let us keep that in mind. God Himself said, as Paul reminds us:

> Wherefore come out from among them, and be ye separate, saith the Lord, . . . and I will receive you, and will be a Father unto you, and ye shall be my sons and daughters (2 Cor. 6:17-18).

Suppose you have ten children healthy and well, and one other child who has scarlet fever. Let that one with scarlet fever go in with the ten that are well, and the one could infect them all. But if you had ten children with scarlet fever and you had one that was healthy, you could not bring the healthy one in and make the other ten well. It does not work that way.

Balaam was a prophet of God back in Old Testament times. Israel was in a big conflict with the Midianites. Both nations were at a standstill so that there was no give or take. Balak the king called Balaam the prophet and asked him to curse Israel. Balaam tried to do it, but he could not do it. He just could not. God would not let him curse Israel. Balaam told Balak that Israel would win out. But then Balaam for the sake of money told Balak what to do, and he did it. He sent his Midianites to make friends of the Israelites. They did, and they infected the Israelites with their own unbelief. And how far that would have gone no one knows, had it not been for Phinehas, that great priest, who came and saw an Israelite man and a Midianite woman together. He speared them through in an act of violence. As a consequence, war broke out, but in the war Israel won the victory.

That is the old recorded event. You may say "that is rough," but it is true. Death is rough. It is also rough to be lost. It is also rough to be away from God. You and I need to remember that this business of becoming a believer in Christ is a matter of life and death. When we are trying to win people, we are trying to save souls from doom. Do we realize that they are going to be lost? There is no halfway measure. The issue is not hanging in doubt. "Whosoever believeth in Him is saved, and whosoever believeth not is condemned already" (John 3). We are not waiting to see how things will turn out. It is all true now. Except they believe in the Lord Jesus Christ, they are all lost.

There is such a danger that we who believe could be like this church at Pergamos. We could hold fast to the name, we could hold fast to our faith even though we died, but we could forfeit our whole advantage by giving in and compromising with these other people according to the doctrine of Balaam.

JUDGMENT UPON PERGAMOS
(Revelation 2:15-17)

We are dealing now with the portion of Revelation in which the Lord Jesus Christ sends messages to the seven churches. This apparently refers to seven different congregations in the general area of Asia that we now call Asia Minor. Doubtless these were actual congregations, and these conditions prevailed among them as John recorded. But I want you to keep in mind that the words that we are reading and considering are not the words of John. This is the revelation that was given to John from the Lord. This is the way the Lord Jesus Christ feels and what He has to say about these churches.

> And to the angel of the church in Pergamos write; These things saith he which hath the sharp sword with two edges (2:12).

Everyone acquainted with Scripture knows that the one thing referred to as being the sharp, two-edged sword is the Bible, the Word of God, "sharper than a two-edged sword, dividing asunder even the bone from the marrow, even the soul from the spirit." That figure is not used about anything else. John tells us in the first chapter that he saw a vision of the Son of man, and out of His mouth went a sharp two-edged sword. This implies the penetrating, revealing, opening function of God's Word. Anyone who reads the Bible slowly, openmindedly, and willingly will be opened up before God. Such a one will be exposed before Him who knows us altogether. "These things saith he which hath the sharp sword with two edges; I know thy works [I understand how you do], and where thou dwellest [I know the associations you keep; I know where you have settled down in your heart and mind], even where Satan's seat is."

Now, there is more in this than I can interpret for us, but I am satisfied that this is one of the most solemn things that can be said to a believer in Christ. It is just possible for a believer in Christ to settle down and dwell where Satan's seat is. There is one thing about Satan that we do well to keep in mind: he is not in hell now. We would be much better off if he were, but that is not where he is. Peter describes the devil as a roaring lion seeking whom he may devour (1 Peter 5:8). It would seem from this Scripture that it is left to the words of the Lord

Jesus Christ to say he can be in church. That is the idea here.

Satan's approach to any believer is through our human nature. He approaches us through the flesh; and the flesh has at
least three avenues of interest: the things that feel good, the
things that look good, and the things that set us up and make
us feel like somebody special. Whatever in the world can we
do about this? Reckon yourself indeed to be dead. There isn't
any other way. "If any man will come after me, let him deny
himself" (Matt. 16:24).

"Thou holdest fast my name." This is a good thing; there is
no criticism about that. The Lord Jesus said, "I recognize
about you people that you are faithful in your relationship to
me. You have given your testimony, you stand by me, and
you have stood there."

"Thou holdest fast my name, and hast not denied my faith."
This was a church that in a time of persecution did not deny
that they believed in the Lord Jesus Christ. "Even in those
days wherein Antipas was my faithful martyr, who was slain
among you, where Satan dwelleth" (Rev. 2:13). Some were
bitterly persecuted and at least one, Antipas, was killed. We
know nothing of him elsewhere in Scripture and, so far as I
know, no one knows anything of him in history or tradition.
This is the only record that I have been able to uncover of this
man Antipas, who was martyred. Nevertheless, the truth is,
matters had reached the place where in that congregation one
lost his life for his faith. But the congregation did not waver.
The congregation stood steadfast. So this was a church that
remained faithful under persecution.

> But I have a few things against thee, because thou hast there
> them that hold the doctrine of Balaam, who taught Balak to cast
> a stumblingblock before the children of Israel, to eat things
> sacrificed unto idols, and to commit fornication (2:14).

The Pergamos congregation was allowing some folks to teach
compromise with worldly things. These people were teaching
the doctrine of Balaam, which is to say it is all right for Israelites and Ishmaelites to be together. It is all right for Israelites
and Midianites to be together. That was the situation back in
the days of Balaam. And in the Pergamos church there were
people who held this doctrine, this view, that "it is all right for
believers in Christ to associate with unbelievers." This was

dangerous. It is proper for believers to be concerned about worldly people. Actually such people may be within the church and would be on believers' hearts; but what needs to be understood is that believers will not help them go the same route of excess in which they are going. That will not help them. Someone may say, "You might have to show that you care for them." That is quite right, and if it will help, the believer might have to walk in the mud—but he must not let his own car get stuck in mud. That might show the other that the believer cares for him, but both would then need help.

> So hast thou also them that hold the doctrine of the Nicolaitans, which thing I hate (2:15).

As we have noted, no one seems to be very clear as to what the doctrine of the Nicolaitans was. There are some good suggestions, and the one that I am impressed to accept is that this was a group of people who had the general idea that some people in the church were the clergy and the rest of the people were the laity. This would mean that there were certain people who had special orders or spiritual authority, and other people who did not. That is brought out because of the word "laitan" with the syllable "lai" which is the same syllable that is the root of the word "laity."

Whoever these Nicolaitans were, their doctrine was something the Lord Jesus Christ hated and the church at Pergamos tolerated. This is what we should consider. It is possible for a believer who is faithful to the name of the Lord Jesus Christ—a person who would not give in under pressure or persecution—to tolerate in association and in his mind a doctrine which the Lord Jesus Christ hates.

> Repent; or else I will come unto thee quickly, and will fight against them with the sword of my mouth (2:16).

The Lord Jesus Christ warned that He would come and fight against them: these two classes of people, the people who hold the doctrine of Balaam, and the people who hold the doctrine of the Nicolaitans. He would fight against them with the sword of His mouth—the Scriptures. The warning to this church is this: if they do not put those people away, they will have a big controversy in their church between people who insist on being scriptural and others who are not scriptural.

In this connection I often wonder whether in our Protestant churches as a whole, we have fully appreciated those faithful people who are concerned and sensitive about departures into false doctrine. I wonder if I am mistaken in the impression I have that today it is unpopular for anyone to find fault with anyone else's doctrine. The general impression seems to be that we should all get together and everyone give a little here and a little there, so that we all can get together and make things work out. The truth is, you cannot give a little here and give a little there on matters that involve such things even as honesty. You cannot give a little here and give a little there on matters that involve integrity. You cannot give a little here and give a little there if matters involve purity. And least of all, you cannot give a little here and give a little there in matters that involve faithfulness to the Lord.

I wonder whether in the Protestant churches we have not almost condemned ourselves in many many places to serious consequences because we shut out of our fellowship people concerned enough about the Lord and about the truth to raise an objection if someone teaches in a Sunday school class something that isn't true.

The Lord looks down on the heart of His church. He stands in the midst of His church, and when He sees His congregation disposed to tolerate doctrine that is unsound, He feels it. And what is true of the congregation is true of us. If we as believers allow things that He hates, He notices it and He tells us to change and to judge ourselves or else He will come and war against us with the sword of His mouth. He will use the Scripture in bringing our judgment sharply to us. This happened in Pergamos. We remember all the good things He said, and all the stirring things, and then we think of this:

> He that hath an ear, let him hear what the Spirit saith unto the churches; To him that overcometh will I give to eat of the hidden manna, and will give him a white stone, and in the stone a new name written, which no man knoweth saving he that receiveth it (2:17).

The person who overcomes these unsound doctrines and maintains himself in truth before God "will I give to eat of the hidden manna, and will give him a white stone, and in the stone a new name written."

THYATIRA
(Revelation 2:18-29)

What the Lord Jesus Christ told the overcomers in Ephesus and those in Smyrna, in Pergamos, then in Thyatira, and in Sardis, Philadelphia, and Laodicea is all one promise. There is one aspect for this church, another aspect for that one, and so on. Each is part of the blessing of God.

In the same way, with each one of these churches, the Lord Jesus Christ is identified in a particular way. To Ephesus He is one kind of person, the One who holds the seven stars in His right hand and walks in the midst of the seven golden candlesticks; to Smyrna, "These things saith the first and the last, which was dead, and is alive"; to Pergamos, "These things saith he which hath the sharp sword with two edges"; and then to Thyatira, "These things saith the Son of God, who hath his eyes like unto a flame of fire, and his feet are like fine brass"; and to Sardis, "These things saith he that hath the seven Spirits of God, and the seven stars"; to Philadelphia, "These things saith he that is holy, he that is true, he that hath the key of David, he that openeth, and no man shutteth; and shutteth, and no man openeth"; and then to Laodicea, "These things saith the Amen, the faithful and true witness, the beginning of the creation of God." These are not seven different persons. This is the same person from seven perspectives.

The same is true with the overcomers. If we read through the messages to those seven churches and note what is said to an overcomer in each case, all this taken together indicates what is going to happen to the faithful believer in Christ. Some of us perhaps even in this past week have passsed through spiritual experiences in which we were alone with God, and in some sense, to some degree, we grew nearer to Him and committed ourselves to Him in a new way. We entered into some new understanding of the Lord Jesus Christ. Actually, what happened to us was that there dawned in our hearts a new appreciation of how we stand with Him and how we belong to Him. A new name was given to us that no one else knows but we who received it.

Now we look at Thyatira.

> And unto the angel of the church in Thyatira write; These
> things saith the Son of God, who hath his eyes like unto a flame
> of fire, and his feet are like fine brass (2:18).

This description is mentioned in the vision that John tells us
about in the first chapter of Revelation.

> I know thy works, and charity, and service, and faith, and thy
> patience, and thy works; and the last to be more than the first
> (2:19)

This was a hard-working church. Look at this list again. "I
know thy works, and charity": what a proper trait for a believer in Christ. "And service": wonderful. "And faith": wonderful. "And thy patience": patience not just from enduring in
the sense that we are longsuffering and forbearing, but patience in the New Testament always means we keep on with
the attitude we have had. Patience holds the idea that we
keep right on, just keep going, going, going. "And thy works;
and the last to be more than the first." This church at Thyatira
was a hard-working church, and they did much.

"Notwithstanding I have a few things against thee." This
brings to our minds that even we who can thank God for
having an inward activity of the spirit, a willingness to work,
to serve, to be charitable to others, to exercise faith and to be
patient in what we are doing—even we—can miss something.

> Notwithstanding I have a few things against thee, because thou
> sufferest that woman Jezebel, which calleth herself a proph-
> etess, to teach and to seduce my servants to commit fornica-
> tion, and to eat things sacrificed unto idols (2:20).

Just like that martyr Antipas of Pergamos, no one now seems
to be sure at all who this woman Jezebel was. We know of the
woman Jezebel in the Old Testament, the wife of Ahab. We
know how she influenced the people back in those days to
introduce Baal worship in Israel. But this does not mean that
she is reincarnated at this time.

There was evidently some woman, probably in this church
in the city of Thyatira, who was called Jezebel because she
functioned the same way as the old Jezebel did—namely, in
the zeal of her error she drew people after her. That Jezebel
in the Old Testament was a good deal more active than her
husband was. She did a lot, all bad, but she was active, and
she had power. And here in Thyatira was this woman who

called herself a prophetess, who was "to teach and to seduce my servants to commit fornication, and to eat things sacrificed unto idols."

In the Scriptures, generally speaking, in this kind of context, I am satisfied that the use of the term "fornication" and "eating things sacrificed unto idols" mean the same thing as fellowshiping with false religious ideas. This could very well deal with social issues also; but I think the context implies at least that this woman was teaching theological ideas that did not originate from Scripture. They did not necessarily originate from her own self, for perhaps she got them from the outside. This matter of sacrificing unto idols is always associated in Scripture with religions other than our own faith. And this the Thyatirans tolerated: "Thou sufferest that woman . . . to teach and to seduce my servants to commit fornication, and to eat things sacrificed unto idols."

> And I gave her space to repent of her fornication; and she repented not. Behold, I will cast her into a bed, and them that commit adultery with her into great tribulation, except they repent of their deeds. And I will kill her children with death; and all the churches shall know that I am he which searcheth the reins and hearts: and I will give unto every one of you according to your works (2:21-23).

I suppose we all know that the word "reins" is an old English word for "kidneys." Now, a reference to the heart like the one here is poetic; but a reference to the kidneys like this does not seem to be poetic. This Scripture means to say, "I am the one that searches the emotions of people"; or, to get a little closer: "I am the one that searches the inner feelings of people." And a completely modern version would state, "I am the one who probes into the subconscious and unconscious elements of your personality." This passage is a way of saying, "I am the one who searches the heart," and we call this a heart-searching truth. In other words, the Lord Jesus Christ is the One who evaluates my inner disposition, and He personally evaluates my inner likes and dislikes.

> . . . And I will give unto every one of you according to your works. But unto you I say, and to the rest in Thyatira, as many as have not this doctrine, and which have not known the depths of Satan, as they speak; I will put upon you none other burden (2:23-24).

As far as I know, this means "I will put upon you no other burden than just staying in that congregation." That is what I think this passage means. "I will place upon you no other burden than to put up with what you have." If we happen to belong to a congregation in which there is teaching going on, tolerated by the church, that we know isn't true, that would be a burden to our souls. I understand and sympathize greatly with those who simply can't take it, but I want to commend to them the idea that for some to stay in that congregation is good and worthwhile.

> But that which ye have already hold fast till I come (2:25).

I want to commend to every one of us believers in Christ that we not be too ready to forsake others simply because they are on the wrong track. If the ground we are standing on is solid, let us stay there. It will not be easy. In this case with this church, Jesus said to them, "Those of you who do not have this doctrine, this false doctrine, I am not going to put any more on you than the burden you have now." And if I understand this correctly, the burden the faithful Thyatirans had right then was living in a place where false teaching was tolerated. And I say one more time, this would be a pain in the soul to any true believer in Christ.

Here was a congregation that tolerated evil things. They tolerated false teaching and were misled. This false doctrine was leading them into affiliations and participation in things that were contrary to God's will. Christ Jesus was saying to the true believers: "I will put upon you none other burden. That which you have already, hold fast till I come."

> And he that overcometh, and keepeth my works unto the end, to him will I give power over the nations: and he shall rule them with a rod of iron; as the vessels of a potter shall they be broken to shivers: even as I received of my Father. And I will give him the morning star. He that hath an ear, let him hear what the Spirit saith unto the churches (2:26-29).

Chapter 3

† † †

SARDIS AND PHILADELPHIA
(Revelation 3:1-10)

The Book of Revelation opens with John's giving us a description of a vision that he had of the Lord Jesus Christ, the living Lord. He had no sooner seen this vision, and become overwhelmed by it so that he fell at the Lord's feet as one dead, than he was told to see and to write what he saw about the things that were true. The next thing he saw was the Son of man, this vision of the Lord Jesus Christ, the living Lord, standing in the midst of seven golden candlesticks.

These seven golden candlesticks represented seven churches, which John then named. As we think of the churches, we have in mind groups of professed believers and their testimonies. The candlestick was to shed light around it. Because natural human beings do not have light in themselves, it is not given to them to shine. But the church is to give light to the community. These believers in Christ, living in this world, letting their light shine out before men, are the candlesticks.

But we discover in our study of this book a sobering insight. The fact is, these candles do not all burn clearly. Some of them flicker. Indeed, the testimony of believers is often found to be blurred because they have in some way or other, in their human fashion, failed to live out the faith they profess. This is what John was given to see.

The Lord Jesus Christ is standing in the midst of His church, and He is interested in the testimony of His church.

56

We mean by this the church as a body, not so much the individual members, although individuals constitute the church. A congregation develops a character. A congregation acquires certain habits of conduct. In some congregations there is a tone of prayer. But we find some other congregations where prayer is something only a few individuals do. The revelation to John discloses that the Lord sees these things and has His judgment of them. John saw and heard the Lord Jesus Christ telling each congregation, "I see you. I know how it goes with you." The Lord clearly points out something that is dangerous to each one, respectively, which could cause them to lose their testimony. As a result, it was possible for any one of them that the candlestick might be taken out of its place.

In chapter 3 of Revelation there is a short message to a church, the church at Sardis. As we read this, we may feel that if we had any reason to be sad before, now we really ought to mourn.

> And unto the angel of the church in Sardis write; These things saith he that hath the seven Spirits of God, and the seven stars; I know thy works, that thou hast a name that thou livest, and art dead (3:1).

What is the popular meaning of a church's being alive? Wouldn't that include such things as good turnouts for Sunday morning service? Wouldn't that include a large company of people perhaps coming to Sunday school or a youth concert? Of course, there wouldn't be many at the evening service. Too often in America, a congregation that has 40 percent of its members attending regularly is counted a good congregation. That is the statistical average. So if two out of five come to church, we have a strong church. This church at Sardis had a reputation that it was alive—but it was dead.

> Be watchful, and strengthen the things which remain, that are ready to die: for I have not found thy works perfect before God (3:2).

No matter how cold and dead a congregation is, the very fact that they have church services, the fact that they have a preacher preaching, the fact that at least the Bible is opened to read a text indicates that they still have some faith and could be revived. This is the thing to remember. "Be watchful, and strengthen the things which remain, that are ready to die: for I have not found thy works perfect before God." This word "perfect" when used here does not mean that the Lord found no fault or blemish. The idea is rather that He did not see their works coming through to completion. For works to be "perfect" means they are brought through to completion. This helps us to understand the trouble with this church at Sardis. They had a name that they lived: this means, no doubt, that they were active and they were great on starting things. But the Lord did not find their works "perfect"; He did not see them completed. They did not go through to the end. They did not produce satisfactory results.

> Remember therefore how thou hast received and heard, and hold fast, and repent (3:3).

This word "repent" means "judge yourself for your own shortcomings and admit them." And, oh! what a wonderful thing it is when a believer in Christ has once and for all found out that he never will be disqualified from the Lord Jesus Christ because he did not perform perfectly. That will never disqualify the believer. What disqualifies him from the Lord Jesus Christ will be his refusal to admit it. As believers in Christ we are dealing with the most patient, the most kind, the most wonderfully able Friend in the whole world, on earth or in heaven: our Lord Jesus Christ is on our side. He knows us altogether. He knows our frame and remembereth that we are but dust. But there is one thing about us He demands in order to be able to deal with us: He wants us to look inward and admit the truth about ourselves, that we simply are not in ourselves adequate. Then when we repent, it is clear we want help. That is what the Lord is waiting for. And that is what this church at Sardis needed.

> Remember therefore how thou hast received and heard, and hold fast, and repent. If therefore thou shalt not watch, I will come on thee as a thief, and thou shalt not know what hour I will come upon thee. Thou hast a few names even in Sardis which have not defiled their garments; and they shall walk with me in white: for they are worthy (3:3-4).

There are some congregations which by common consent we would say are spiritually dead, but who have a few people among them who will have shining robes in the presence of the Lord because of their faithfulness. If by any chance, any one of you has a kind of dull inward sickening feeling that something like this is true of your congregation—that they are not spiritually alive—I want to tell you that you have an opportunity in that very situation to earn the white robe in the presence of the Lord Jesus Christ. "And they shall walk with me in white: for they are worthy."

> He that overcometh, the same shall be clothed in white raiment; and I will not blot out his name out of the book of life, but I will confess his name before my Father, and before his angels (3:5).

By contrast with Sardis, we come to the message to the church at Philadelphia with not one single criticism.

> And to the angel of the church in Philadelphia write; These things saith he that is holy, he that is true, he that hath the key of David, he that openeth, and no man shutteth; and shutteth, and no man openeth; I know thy works: behold, I have set before thee an open door, and no man can shut it: for thou hast a little strength, and hast kept my word, and hast not denied my name. Behold, I will make them of the synagogue of Satan, which say they are Jews, and are not, but do lie; behold, I will make them to come and worship before thy feet, and to know that I have loved thee. Because thou hast kept the word of my patience, I also will keep thee from the hour of temptation, which shall come upon all the world, to try them that dwell upon the earth (3:7-10).

This passage is somewhat differently interpreted by different students. Some hold that this phrase "thou hast a little strength" is by way of a mild implied criticism, but I wonder if that is not harsh. I am so glad that not all biblical scholars agree with that, for then I have the liberty in my spirit to feel the way I do. I have a feeling that this is an example of a church that wasn't strong for good reasons. Maybe they did not have many members. Maybe their members did not have much money. Maybe there were few people with spare time to give to the church. Maybe these people did not have much learning. Maybe they did not have outstanding leadership. Maybe this was just one of those congregations that had been started in an area where there were few people, and the congregation was weak and small. Perhaps they could not attract a good preacher. They just kept themselves going along the best they knew how. Something like this may be the meaning of "Thou hast a little strength."

I am not sure we should interpret that phrase as a comment of criticism. It seems to me from the rest of these messages to churches that when the Lord wanted to criticize, He made it plain. When He wanted to say something in judgment, He didn't make people guess; He said, for example, "I have something against thee." But that is not how He speaks of this church at Philadelphia. He says, "I have set before thee an open door." These people were going to have an opportunity to witness. No one would be able to stop them from having it: "no man can shut it: for thou hast a little strength, and hast kept my word." This congregation exercised what little strength they had. Maybe they did not have profound preachers or profound Bible teachers, but they had some genuine faith in the Lord and they kept His Word—"and hast not denied my name."

Then the Lord said, "I will make them of the synagogue of Satan." We remember how that was referred to earlier: "which say they are Jews, and are not." I do not think this necessarily refers only to people who physically speaking were Jews. I think that can also refer to people who claim to be religious, who claim to know something of God.

Somehow Christ was going to make this church at Philadelphia a witness, and He was going to so magnify this church in the community around it. Then people who opposed it and people who claimed to be much stronger than they would eventually have to come and admit that the little church had "it." That little church was the real thing. "Because thou hast kept the word of my patience, I also will keep thee from the hour of temptation": what a wonderful message we can pick from that! If any person should feel that he is not a strong believer, that after all is said and done there is no prospect of his ever amounting to anything outstanding as a believer in Christ, would he admit that he had a little strength? Does he believe in the Lord Jesus Christ as his Savior? Does he really and truly believe that Christ died for him? Is he trusting the Lord to save his soul? Is he sure in his heart that God is his and that God is going to keep him? Does he have that much? Even if he has doubts, the truth is that if he will just be patient, if he will cling to Christ when he cannot see, if he will continue to trust in Christ when he does not see how it is going to work out, if he has done his best in following Christ, this precious promise is for him: "I will keep thee from the hour of temptation, which shall come upon all the world, to try them that dwell upon the earth." That person will be blessed.

LAODICEA
(Revelation 3:11-22)

> Behold, I come quickly: hold that fast which thou hast, that no man take thy crown (3:11).

There is not a single person who ever heard the gospel of the Lord Jesus Christ and believed in Him that did not have something. He should hold that fast. Does he really believe Jesus is Christ? He should hold to it. Does he believe Christ died for sinners? He should hold that. Does he understand he is a sinner? He should hold that. Can he believe that Christ died for him? "Hold that fast which thou hast, that no man take thy crown." He should let no one weaken his grip. He should never let any suggestion from anywhere cause him to doubt Christ, who gave Himself for him. And as surely as that person will keep the word of the Lord's patience, continuing to believe all the way through, this will be true:

> Him that overcometh will I make a pillar in the temple of my God, and he shall go no more out: and I will write upon him the name of my God, and the name of the city of my God, which is new Jerusalem, which cometh down out of heaven from my God: and I will write upon him my new name (3:12).

And who is going to qualify for this? Someone who simply holds fast what he knows about the Lord Jesus Christ.

We have come to the last of the churches in this portion of Revelation, and I approach this last message with much uneasiness. I have these feelings because I fear that in speaking forthrightly, it will be almost impossible for me not to appear to condemn personally so many of my fellow believers.

> And unto the angel of the church of the Laodiceans write;
> These things saith the Amen, the faithful and true witness, the
> beginning of the creation of God; I know thy works, that thou
> art neither cold nor hot: I would thou wert cold or hot. So then
> because thou art lukewarm, and neither cold nor hot, I will
> spew thee out of my mouth (3:14-16).

I fear I cannot do justice to this. In my own heart I feel this is
the most awful word in the Bible. This is the Lord Jesus
Christ speaking. The one thing about us that He cannot and
will never tolerate is for us to be lukewarm. And how easy it is
to be lukewarm! How easy it is to have just enough activity so
as to lull our consciences, and not so much activity to hurt us.
The Lord can put up with our mistakes, but He will not put
up with our indifference.

> Because thou sayest, I am rich, and increased with goods, and
> have need of nothing; and knowest not that thou art wretched,
> and miserable, and poor, and blind, and naked: I counsel thee
> to buy of me gold tried in the fire, that thou mayest be rich; and
> white raiment, that thou mayest be clothed, and that the
> shame of thy nakedness do not appear; and anoint thine eyes
> with eyesalve, that thou mayest see (3:17-18).

"I counsel thee" means giving advice, and the advice consists
of three things "to buy of me gold tried in the fire, that thou
mayest be rich" (faith tried in the fire); "and white raiment,
that thou mayest be clothed" (the white raiment of Christ's
righteousness, the white raiment spoken of to the church of
Sardis, faithfulness); "and that the shame of thy nakedness do
not appear" (getting under the righteousness of the Lord
Jesus Christ). The writer adds, "And anoint thine eyes with
eyesalve, that thou mayest see" (don't be so blind).

> As many as I love, I rebuke and chasten: be zealous therefore,
> and repent (3:19).

This is the only place in this whole revelation about the
churches where Christ expresses rebuke without praise. This
is the only church of the seven for which not one good thing
is said. Just as with Philadelphia there was no blame, so
with Laodicea there is no praise. It was a strong church, a
wealthy church. They thought they had everything, but they
had nothing. Now the Lord tells them, "As many as I love, I
rebuke and chasten: be zealous therefore, and repent." There

is safety in zeal. I know that zealous people are sometimes annoying; they can be disturbing. But that reaction is for us to think about. The truth is that the person who takes things to heart, and acts on them so that he gets on fire about something, is a lot safer than the person who takes it easy.

Just as I do not know anything worse than verse 16, so I do not for the moment know of anything that is more wonderful than verse 20. This verse is often quoted as Christ's invitation to come to Him.

> Behold, I stand at the door, and knock: if any man hear my voice, and open the door, I will come in to him, and will sup with him, and he with me (3:20).

This was said to the church at Laodicea. This was said to a church that had not one good thing said of it in the presence of God. But our Lord Jesus Christ is just that humble and meek. He will not take offense. If anyone at any time had lived any length of time in such inconsequential state as never to do anything, or never to amount to a thing, do we realize what the Lord wants of him? "I stand at the door, and knock: if any man hear my voice, and open the door"—if any lukewarm person will open his heart—"I will come in to him, and will sup with him, and he with me." He will not have to run. He will not have to climb. He will not have to work. He will not even have to suffer. All in the world he has to do is to open his heart and let the Lord Jesus Christ come in. Other things will follow. This is the beginning.

So if anyone by any chance should have this feeling, here is the message for him. He should open his heart. The Lord is standing at the heart's door and knócking. And when the Lord Jesus Christ comes in, the person will not have to turn on any lights: the Lord will be the light.

This is one of the most wonderful things about the Lord Jesus Christ: in His meekness He even cares about the people who do not care about Him. And as long as they do not let Him in, there is no hope for them. Despite the fact He died for them, there will be people going right straight on out to sea and being lost. This can happen despite the fact the Lord Jesus Christ gave His life for them. Some will miss the blessing of God simply because they never opened their heart's door to the living Lord Jesus Christ.

Chapter 4

† † †

AN OPEN DOOR TO HEAVEN
(Revelation 4:1-4)

In Revelation 4, the scene changes. The reader's attention is shifted from earth, where the church is now, to heaven, where God is. Heaven is incomprehensible to us in many ways. The Scriptures say of the believer in heaven, "It doth not yet appear what we shall be like." There is no specific line-by-line description of heaven anywhere in the Bible. When you and I think, we use categories of time and space: a thing is from here to there, being that long; it is from now till then, with that much time involved. In heaven there is no time, because it is eternal; there is no space, because it is infinite. When time and space are left out, we cannot think. And that is the reason why, if we were to see heaven, we could not tell about it.

When Paul told about one who had been caught up "into the third heaven," he said that person saw things it was not possible for him to utter (2 Cor. 12:2-4). One reason why no one has described heaven is because there are no words in our human vocabulary to describe it.

The Book of Revelation reports that John looked up into heaven, but the Lord does not give John a new vocabulary. He does not give John new terms and ideas with which to describe what he sees. If John had been given a glimpse of heaven as it is, he would have been left speechless. There would have been no adequate words to utter. All he would have had was probably the immediate sensation of joy and

delight, but there would have been no word about it, because
he could not have had a thing to say. Yet the Lord Jesus Christ
gave to John in this vision a revelation in symbols of what is in
heaven.

> After this I looked, and, behold, a door was opened in
> heaven . . . (4:1).

The implication seems to be that for the moment he was out of
his trance, as it were, out of that state of ecstasy he experienced in the vision, so that he was probably very much in his
normal frame of mind. "And, behold, a door was opened in
heaven." This was the beginning of the vision. A door opening
is a way of letting a person look into something. When the
door is open, we can look inside.

> . . . and the first voice which I heard was as it were of a trum-
> pet talking with me . . . (4:1).

The trumpet is an instrument used in battle because its
piercing notes will rise above the din and the clash and the
clamor of warfare. I suppose no note will carry as far as a
trumpet blast. It has a penetrating, far-reaching tone. John
heard a voice like a trumpet. This is to say that when John had
the sensation of this voice talking to him, he felt a challenging,
penetrating, powerful, clear commanding tone of a voice like
a trumpet. We are reminded that at the voice of the trumpet,
the dead will rise from the graves.

> And the first voice which I heard was as it were of a trumpet
> talking with me; which said, Come up hither, and I will show
> thee things which must be hereafter. And immediately I was in
> the spirit . . . (4:1-2).

Now, when John says "immediately I was in the spirit," it
seems to be a case of his being given a vision. He was not
given the vision to a cold mind; he was inwardly so enthralled
and so inflamed in spirit that he was able to see things and
understand them far beyond his ordinary understanding.

> . . . And, behold, a throne was set in heaven (4:2).

John has not mentioned the throne until now. When the
vision was located down here on earth, John saw seven
candlesticks: that was the church. In the midst of the seven
candlesticks was the living Lord: that was the living Lord in

His church. There is no throne on earth on which the Lord sits: He is not Boss of this world. This is the reason we have all the trouble we do. This is the reason we are in the danger we are in. He is not Boss in this world. And more than that, there is no throne down here to place Him on apart from the throne in our hearts. There is none anywhere else on which we could put Him. His throne is in heaven. Note that when John reports on looking up and seeing the door open so that he can gaze into heaven, the first thing he sees is a throne. That symbolizes control. And here is a marvelous truth: all things in the world, in our lives, for time and eternity, are under control; there is a throne. This world may look as if it is running fast and loose, but it is not. Many in the world may seem to be running that way, but their time is limited. There is a great deal going on for which God is not responsible; but to the extent to which it goes, He is responsible. He is responsible for how long it will last.

Many things are happening that God did not cause to come to pass. But He will certainly cause them to come to an end, because He has veto power. God sets the bounds of the sea: thus far the ocean will go and no further. The waves may roll as high as they will, but they will come up just so far and they will go back whence they came. And this is because God has structured the coastline the way He did. No water can rise above it. And so with men. The heathen may rage, ungodly men may rise to all heights of temper and ambition, but their days are numbered and their stride is measured. There is One on the throne.

Believers in Christ need never be greatly disturbed about how things are happening. Someone may say, "Well, it might kill me." So what? "It is appointed unto man once to die." So far as we are concerned, we all die. Sooner or later we will come to it and die. It is no small matter, no light matter, and I do not want you to think I am even smiling about it. But I can say this, that you and I as believers in Christ ought to get used to the idea. There is nothing for us to cringe from as far as death is concerned. Death has lost its sting; the grave has lost its victory (1 Cor. 15:55).

We are sorry to lose our loved ones. We do not like our homes to be broken up. We do not like fellowship to be disrupted. But all that is a far cry from being afraid of death. We may shrink from it. Humanly speaking, we may fear it. But Jesus of Nazareth passed through it. The way is open.

As far as this whole world is concerned, it may be just as jumbled and seething and tumbling as the waves of the sea, but in heaven there is a throne. I assure you that the throne is not shaking. John saw a throne set in heaven, and One sat on the throne. We should never let the echo of this get out of our souls. God is, and God is on the throne. We can hold to that. And that confidence will be the beginning of peace in our souls. When God is on the throne, every interest we have is safe in Him. We can trust Him.

> And he that sat was to look upon like a jasper and a sardine stone . . . (4:3).

These are precious stones. This means there was glory in it. This Person on the throne was glorious.

> . . . and there was a rainbow round about the throne, in sight like unto an emerald (4:3).

We all know the distinctive thing about a rainbow—all the colors. Colors make for beauty. Because this is in Scripture, the rainbow may imply promise. We remember the rainbow in the cloud in Noah's time, after the Flood. God gave His word. Perhaps the rainbow around the throne implies that the One sitting there is One who keeps His word. It is a good thought in any case. But I suspect that this primarily means glory beyond description. All the beauty we could ever imagine was seen around the throne that John was looking upon. And the throne was "in sight like unto an emerald."

Jasper, sardine, and emerald evidently were very precious and beautiful stones in John's day. John had seen this precious, glorious, shining, wonderful sight and One on that throne, brilliant in His glory. And then:

> And round about the throne were four and twenty seats: and upon the seats I saw four and twenty elders sitting, clothed in white raiment; and they had on their heads crowns of gold (4:4).

The word "crown" used here is a word that could have been translated "wreath." This was the kind of a crown given in those Roman times to people who were victors in any contest.

In the Olympic games, when someone would struggle almost unto death to win some athletic contest, the reward was always to be crowned with a wreath of olive leaves. Being crowned with this wreath implied the highest honor. And these crowns which John saw were wreaths, as if they were symbols of achievement. They could have been symbols of an overcoming victory that these people had experienced.

John saw twenty-four elders sitting on these twenty-four seats, but let us not try to name these twenty-four, and let us not try to figure out why there were just exactly twenty-four. We would do well to leave the number element out of our thinking at this time. We may remember how we noted that twelve could represent the total of anything on earth. Thus this would seem to be the total of God's people on earth.

Most of the commentators I have consulted suggest that the twenty-four seem to take into account the twelve sons of Jacob in the Old Testament and the twelve apostles in the New. There is some thought here that John saw the saints of the Old Testament and the saints of the New Testament, the twelve tribes of Israel and the twelve apostles.

In any case, these leaders were sitting clothed in white raiment. White raiment is just exactly what it means to anyone anywhere—clean. And there is no one who knows human nature at all who would not perceive that if he were clean, it would mean he had been cleansed. As surely as he were human he would not be clean. If those persons in heaven now are in white raiment, someone cleansed them. We should not overlook the fact that this is our prospect. When we get to heaven, we will be clothed in white raiment. Our clothing will be given to us. To the ladies I suggest that you will be provided with a trousseau. I am sure that in your patient waiting, while you are down here, you would like to stitch a few fine threads on it. But the robe will be the robe of the righteousness of the Lord Jesus Christ. Some of us men who can get awfully grimy living in this world—and are believers in Christ—face the prospect of being in the presence of God without spot and without wrinkle in white raiment.

"And they had on their heads crowns of gold." In Revelation 2:10 we read, "Be thou faithful unto death, and I will give thee a crown of life." This would be a crown of gold.

THE GLORY OF THE THRONE
(Revelation 4:5-11)

> And out of the throne proceeded lightnings and thunderings
> and voices . . . (4:5).

Whatever this means to you, it certainly is impressive, isn't it? "Lightnings and thunderings and voices." This aspect of the vision brings to John's consciousness the impression of unlimited power. Have any of you had the experience of being in a really violent electrical storm? In Canada, where I lived as a lad, we had storms in which when that thunder cracked, we thought all the branches would fall off the trees. As a boy I was scared. The way that lightning would flash and that thunder would roll was frightening. Here John is looking up into heaven. Lightnings and thunderings and voices were coming out from this throne. Whatever other impression this makes on your mind, one thing is sure: that throne was no mere picture. It was not just something to look at.

The throne seemed to be the center of almighty power. This is the impression it made upon John.

> . . . And there were seven lamps of fire burning before the
> throne, which are the seven Spirits of God (4:5).

Though John wrote of the seven Spirits of God, I do not feel this means there were the Holy Spirit and six others. I think it is a way of bringing to our minds the total Spirit of God. Just as those seven congregations in Revelation 1–3 were the one church in seven aspects. We have noted that when the number seven is mentioned, it means the whole, the total thing. This would mean here, then, that the whole Spirit of God was there before the throne in flaming fire.

> And before the throne there was a sea of glass like unto crystal
> (4:6).

I do not know that anyone has a suggestion to offer as to why the "sea of glass" should be there unless it were just to increase the glory. The crystal increases and enhances by reflection the light that has shone. Let us think of that throne so brilliant, and the One on the throne, as brilliant gems: the throne itself like a great emerald, and in front of the throne seven Spirits with seven flames of fire rising in front. And all around in front a whole sea of burnished glass. This gives the impression it was all just beyond words in its brilliant light, in that glory that was surrounding the throne. We have some idea from this of the glory of the presence of God, as it was given to John.

> . . . And in the midst of the throne, and round about the
> throne, were four beasts full of eyes before and behind (4:6).

With language like this, speaking of "in the midst of the throne, and round about the throne," there is the impression that the throne was not something solid, like a piece of carpentry work. This seems to mean that the sovereign control by God is symbolized in this way by the throne. And now John was to see that right there in the very presence, as well as in the very essence of this, there were four beasts full of eyes in front and in back. No doubt, at this point many persons would tend to stop reading the Book of Revelation. Here they would just check out.

But let us look at what we have here. It is possible that the word "beast" is not the happiest English translation of what John wrote. Perhaps "living creatures" would be better. This uses two words, both longer, but could mean the same thing. John saw that there were creatures, full of eyes before and behind. This brings something to John's consciousness. Eyes see. The idea of creatures that have eyes before and behind—as every five-year-old boy thinks his mother has— suggests that they see everything. Thus these four creatures would be conscious of everything that is. Since there were four, it would seem they see everything there is. These four living creatures would be conscious of all that is. It has been suggested that since four is the earthly number, and the four living creatures could refer to the whole of creation, in a sense they symbolize the whole of creation with the total consciousness of the created world.

But there is something more about these living creatures.

> And the first beast was like a lion, and the second beast like a
> calf, and the third beast had a face as a man, and the fourth
> beast was like a flying eagle (4:7).

These four representations—a lion, a calf, a man, and an eagle—may seem strange. But these four are mentioned in the Book of Ezekiel. These are the four creatures which Ezekiel saw in his vision of the sovereignty of God. Ezekiel saw God on the throne, God providentially over the whole mixed-up confusion on earth. Always there was God, this great Being. Ezekiel saw the glory of God by the river Chebar.

Some say that the lion suggests strength, and this could be so understood. The calf or the ox suggests patience, since certainly the ox is known as a patient beast. A man suggests intelligence. An eagle connotes swiftness. And so it has been suggested that John's vision saw creation at its very best, in all its strength, in all its patience, in all its intelligence, in all its promptness to act. This is one way of interpreting the passage.

Now let us consider the four Gospels. The Gospels have individual characteristics; they can be seen as four different pictures of the same Person. Matthew presents more about Christ as King than any of the others. In Mark the emphasis is upon the Servant, the working Person. This is another aspect of the Lord Jesus Christ: He was a great Servant. The various aspects of the humanity of Christ are seen in the Gospel according to Luke. In John there is more about His deity, more about Jesus of Nazareth as the Son of God. Thus the four Gospels show Him as King, as Servant, as Man, and as the Son of God. Some see the King as the lion, the king of beasts. They see the Servant as the ox, the patient beast of burden. The Son of man they see as the man. The Son of God, high and overseeing all things, they see in the symbol of the eagle. In any case, these four characterizations are strikingly enough common to Scripture, and their tone is common to Scripture. They seem to represent four aspects of created reality.

> And the four beasts had each of them six wings about him; and they were full of eyes within: and they rest not day and night, saying, Holy, holy, holy, Lord God Almighty, which was, and is, and is to come (4:8).

Bible students will recognize the creatures with six wings. In the sixth chapter of the Book of Isaiah, where Isaiah relates his vision of the glory of God, the seraphim were all round about Him. They had six wings, and with two they covered their face—their eyes—so that they would not look on His glory. With two they covered their feet that He might not see their humiliation. And with two they could fly, to obey Him. That is one aspect of the truth. In Isaiah the seraphim said, "Holy, holy, holy, is the Lord of hosts: the whole earth is full of his glory." Here in Revelation the beasts are saying the same, but there is something added that isn't in the Isaiah passage: "which was, and is, and is to come."

> And when those beasts give glory and honor and thanks to him that sat on the throne, who liveth for ever and ever, the four and twenty elders fall down before him that sat on the throne, and worship him that liveth for ever and ever, and cast their crowns before the throne, saying, Thou art worthy, O Lord, to receive glory and honor and power: for thou hast created all things, and for thy pleasure they are and were created (4:9-11).

This seems to be a gesture of saying, "Any honor we have ever achieved is all thine. Any honor that has ever come to us just does not belong to us at all. Everything that has ever come to us belongs to thee." They take their crowns and cast them before the throne, saying, "Thou art worthy, O Lord, to receive glory and honor and power: for thou hast created all things, and for thy pleasure they are and were created." This chapter concludes with great praise to God as Creator.

Chapters 5 and 6

† † †

THE LAMB ON THE THRONE
(Revelation 5:1-10)

> And I saw in the right hand of him that sat on the throne a book
> written within and on the backside, sealed with seven seals. And
> I saw a strong angel proclaiming with a loud voice, Who is
> worthy to open the book, and to loose the seals thereof? And no
> man in heaven, nor in earth, neither under the earth, was able to
> open the book, neither to look thereon (5:1-3).

The Book of Revelation may be taken to convey to us, as in a
sense it seems to symbolize, the projected will of God. It is
almost as though in this book there were sketched out God's
plan for His whole creation. The fact that the book John saw
was sealed with seven seals implies that the contents were
unknown. Readers can have in mind that the will of God for
the future is unknown. In truth, the will of God for the world
is unknown. The book was sealed with seven seals. Over and
over again the number seven implies the total idea. This book
was totally sealed; its contents were totally hidden from men.
They were totally unknown, but known to God. This could be
what God's will really entails as far as this world is concerned.

Then came this question, Who is going to be willing or
ready to open this book? That is to say, Who will take responsibility for achieving the will of God on earth? No man in
heaven or in earth or under the earth was able to open the
book, neither to look into it. It would seem that what John
sees in this moment is that the will of God is beyond human
capacity to perform.

> And I wept much, because no man was found worthy to open
> and to read the book, neither to look thereon (5:4)

John was affected, profoundly stirred by the weakness of man.

73

No man was found worthy to open the book and read it.

> And one of the elders saith unto me, Weep not: behold, the
> Lion of the tribe of Judah, the Root of David, hath prevailed to
> open the book, and to loose the seven seals thereof (5:5).

Someone from among the men on the face of the earth, one of
the children of Israel, the Lion of the tribe of Judah, the One
who the Old Testament prophecies referred to, Someone
coming from the tribe of Judah would reign as a lion does
among the beasts of the forest and the beasts of the field.
"Behold, the Lion of the tribe of Judah, the Root of David."
Here again attention is drawn to Old Testament Scriptures
that a Root would come out of David—a person sometimes
called a Branch and sometimes a Root. "Hath prevailed to
open the book, and to loose the seven seals thereof."

> And I beheld, and, lo, in the midst of the throne and of the four
> beasts, and in the midst of the elders, stood a Lamb as it had
> been slain . . . (5:6).

Despite the contrast here, we may be sure John is not writing
this just for affect. This actually happened to John. This is
what was given to John to see. This particular word for "a
lamb" is used in only one other place in the New Testament; it
means "a little lamb." When Jesus of Nazareth was talking to
Peter after the Resurrection, He asked him three times,
"Lovest thou me?" Peter replied, "Yea, Lord, thou knowest
that I love thee." "Feed my lambs" (John 21:15-17). That is
the only other place in the New Testament where this word
translated "little lamb" is used. It was a little Lamb, and that
is what John saw. And not only that, but John saw this Lamb
as it had been slain, with a scar from having been killed.

> . . . Having seven horns and seven eyes, which are the seven
> Spirits of God sent forth into all the earth. And he came and
> took the book out of the right hand of him that sat upon the
> throne (5:6-7).

This Lamb had seven horns and seven eyes, which John tells
us "are the seven Spirits of God." We need to remember that
what John saw was a symbol, with the number seven meaning
total. The expression "the seven Spirits of God" means the
Holy Spirit in completeness. Something like this was stated in
Isaiah 11:2 and was mentioned in chapter 1 of Revelation. The

idea is mentioned here again. The word "horn" in the symbolism of the Bible refers to power and strength. For instance, there is the horn of Assyria and the horn of Babylon and the horn of the Gentiles. Thus reference is made to the power of these creatures, these beings, these persons. This Lamb with seven horns has perfect power, all power.

In this context let us call to mind the Great Commission.

> . . . All power is given unto me in heaven and in earth. Go ye therefore, and teach all nations (Matt. 28:18-19).

This statement fits in with what John saw, this Lamb all powerful. Now the meaning of the seven eyes can be grasped when it is remembered that the eye is that with which we see, with which we understand. Seven eyes means total seeing, total understanding, knowing all things. Thus this Lamb, this almighty power, knowing all things (filled with the Holy Spirit), was "sent forth into all the earth."

When John saw this Lamb, he saw this Being had all power, all wisdom, and the Holy Spirit of God in Him. And to John—who lived with Jesus of Nazareth, walked with Him, saw Him live and die and be raised again from the dead, and saw Him go to glory—this is the One whom he sees in this vision. This is the Lamb, emphasizing and accenting His approach as He comes to do the will of God.

Here is an amazing thing for us to learn. The very secret to doing the will of God is to yield like a lamb into His will. The Lamb is innocent and pure and has no personal strength or violence. It was recorded about Jesus of Nazareth that when He was reviled, He reviled not again. Neither was any violence found in His mouth. When He was beset upon by His enemies, He raised no hand in self-defense. When Peter would have fought for Him, He made Peter put up his sword and told him, "How else is the will of God to be done?" He told Peter, "Thinkest thou that I cannot now pray to my Father, and he shall presently give me twelve legions of angels? But how then shall the scriptures be fulfilled?" (Matt. 26:51-54; see John 18:10-11). The truth is that the word of God is fulfilled in this way, as a Lamb would do.

I often wonder, How long must a believer live and how much must he learn until he can get this grounded into his bones, that the way for him to achieve God's purpose is to be humble and meek as a lamb, yielding to the will of God? That is the cue, as it always will be. John saw it in heaven.

This book of the will of God, this total plan of God's purpose about the whole creation—who can read it? A Lamb. And a Lamb that is slain. But that very Lamb that is slain is the One who has power, wisdom, and the Spirit of God.

> And he came and took the book out of the right hand of him that sat upon the throne. And when he had taken the book, the four beasts and four and twenty elders fell down before the Lamb, having every one of them harps, and golden vials full of odors, which are the prayers of saints (5:7-8).

Harps, of course, are for making beautiful music. When we note the golden vials full of odors—the prayers of the saints—we think of those twenty-four elders representing the believing people of the Old and New Testament times, being all God's people out of a ready and willing heart coming to give praise to the Lamb, carrying their flasks of precious perfume which are the prayers of the saints. Here we do well to have in mind that when, as believers in Christ, we thank God or trust God or turn to God in praise, we put a little perfume in the flask. It happens to the praise and the glory of His name. This is good for our souls. It glorifies God. God is pleased to hear our praise because every such expression of appreciation from the heart is kept in a little container that will be given to the Lamb who is worthy of all praise for what He has done for us.

> And they sung a new song, saying, Thou art worthy to take the book, and to open the seals thereof: for thou wast slain, and hast redeemed us to God by thy blood out of every kindred; and tongue, and people, and nation; and hast made us unto our God kings and priests: and we shall reign on the earth (5:9-10).

We do well at this point to remember that the Lamb does not suffer because He likes suffering. The Lamb does not suffer because of a lack of strength. The Lamb suffers because that is the only way to save me. He suffered for me because that was the only way to save me. Paul pointed out that if righteousness could have come in any other way than by the grace of God in Christ Jesus, then Christ Jesus died in vain (Gal. 2:21). The point Paul emphasizes in his Galatian letter is that salvation comes no other way. Righteousness does not come in any other way than as a gift to us, because Christ Jesus died for us. He has become our righteousness by dying for us. Throughout all the eternal ages, His name will be praised.

> . . . For thou wast slain, and hast redeemed us to God by thy blood out of every kindred and tongue, and people, and nation; and hast made us unto our God kings and priests: and we shall reign on the earth (5:9-10).

In the King James Version, which I am quoting here, it reads "kings and priests." It appears that a closer translation of the Greek brings out the phrase "a kingdom of priests." In any case, the idea of both kings and priests is in this passage. We should not miss the point. The king is the one in authority and control. The priest is the one who serves God. Believers in Christ in one sense are to be kings inasmuch as they are to be in authority and in control over themselves. They are also priests in that they serve Christ. Every single believer in Christ is called to be a member of the kingdom of priests. Each is to serve God on behalf of others.

"And we shall reign on the earth." This does not mean believers will be surrounded with earthly pageantry, as human kings are, or that they will be decked out with all the glory of Solomon, in that sense of reigning as an oriental monarch. This expression means we will get the job done in our obedience here on earth. Believers will win out.

THE SONG OF THE LAMB
(Revelation 5:11-6:8)

> And I beheld, and I heard the voice of many angels round about the throne and the beasts and the elders: and the number of them was ten thousand times ten thousand, and thousands of thousands (5:11).

Let us remember about the symbol "thousand." Ten seems to be the complete earthly form of anything. Ten fingers and ten toes are all there is in a man. The Ten Commandments are the will of God on earth. Ten times ten times ten makes a thousand. When we think of ten in length, and ten in breadth,

and ten in height, it is like saying a thousand. Thus the complete will of God would be "a thousand." Now, imagine ten
thousand. When the Word of God says "the cattle on a
thousand hills are His," this means on all the hills (Ps. 50:10).
When the Scripture says, "One day is with the Lord as a
thousand years, and a thousand years is as one day," the
meaning is not numbering the days on a calendar (2 Peter
3:8). That Scripture means "all time."

Then what is implied by ten thousand? It means just everything. And what about ten thousand times ten thousand? And
if that were not enough, thousands of thousands. This is an
expression that means the same as "the sand by the
seashore"—innumerable. This would mean the same as "the
stars of the heavens"—a multitude. And this is what we have
when John reports, "I heard the voice of many angels round
about the throne and the beasts and the elders: and the
number of them was ten thousand times ten thousand, and
thousands of thousands." This means the whole creation on
earth and in heaven. John then tells what he heard in heaven,
and one will never find a stronger, louder, sweeter song than
this one. This is the song of the Lamb.

> Worthy is the Lamb that was slain to receive power, and
> riches, and wisdom, and strength, and honour, and glory, and
> blessing. And every creature which is in heaven, and on the
> earth, and under the earth, and such as are in the sea, and all
> that are in them, heard I saying, Blessing and honour, and
> glory, and power, be unto him that sitteth upon the throne,
> and unto the Lamb for ever and ever (5:12-13).

My attention has been drawn to the fact that in the Greek all
this is recorded in a way that is impossible to put into English.
The definite article is before each one of these four words.
Literally translated this would be "the" blessing and "the"
honor and "the" glory and "the" power, as if in each case it
would be the highest of all blessings and the highest of all
honor and the highest of all glory and the highest of all power
"unto him that sitteth upon the throne [that is, God], and
unto the Lamb for ever and ever."

> And the four beasts said, Amen. And the four and twenty
> elders fell down and worshiped him that liveth for ever and
> ever (5:14).

What a mighty, tremendous, uplifting experience John had when he looked into heaven and saw all creation lifting up a mighty paean of triumphal song to the Lamb that was slain. This was written in a day when the church was on the verge of being severely persecuted. It was a day when John himself was a prisoner in exile. It was a day when a Roman emperor sat on the throne and called himself god. And by the power of his soldiers the emperor was putting down all opposition, and by the manner of his dealing in violence and in terrifying the people he sought to silence every voice around him. This was written in a day when to confess that one was a believer in Christ was to risk his life. Oh! that it were possible for believers when they worship in their church services to have their eyes opened to see so they were able one more time to understand and to grasp that it is the name of the Lord Jesus Christ Himself that is lifted above every name. God has willed that all praise and honor shall come to that name! God has given Christ Jesus a name above every name so that "at the name of Jesus every knee should bow, . . . and every tongue should confess that Jesus Christ is Lord, to the glory of God the Father" (Phil. 2:10-11).

> And I saw when the Lamb opened one of the seals, and I heard, as it were the noise of thunder, one of the four beasts saying, Come and see. And I saw, and behold a white horse: and he that sat on him had a bow; and a crown was given unto him: and he went forth conquering, and to conquer. And when he had opened the second seal, I heard the second beast say, Come and see. And there went out another horse that was red: and power was given to him that sat thereon to take peace from the earth, and that they should kill one another: and there was given unto him a great sword. And when he had opened the third seal, I heard the third beast say, Come and see. And I beheld, and lo a black horse; and he that sat on him had a pair of balances in his hand. And I heard a voice in the midst of the four beasts say, A measure of wheat for a penny, and three measures of barley for a penny; and see thou hurt not the oil and the wine. And when he had opened the fourth seal, I heard the voice of the fourth beast say, Come and see. And I looked, and behold a pale horse: and his name that sat on him was Death, and Hell followed with him. And power was given unto them over the fourth part of the earth, to kill with sword, and with hunger, and with death, and with the beasts of the earth (6:1-8).

Here is introduced in John's vision the scene commonly called "the four horsemen of the Apocalypse." They are distinguished by individual colors: the white horse, the red horse, the black horse, and the pale horse. These horses are mentioned in Zechariah. Matthew 24 presents something very close to this.

The common judgment among Bible students is that this first one—the white horse going forth "conquering, and to conquer"—suggests Christ Jesus in the Gospels. This could imply the release of the gospel on the face of the earth. White is very often associated with the Lord. The passage records that a crown was given to Him, and He went forth conquering and to conquer. This triumphant figure would seem to be suggestive of spreading the gospel through the earth.

The second horse, the red one, is commonly held to represent war on the earth. The third horse, which is black, unquestionably suggests famine. The fourth horse, the pale one, seems to represent death: "And power was given unto them over the fourth part of the earth, to kill with sword, and with hunger, and with death, and with the beasts of the earth." This seems to include reference to pestilence or calamity.

All this seems to be a strange combination. But in Matthew 24, when it states that the gospel has been released in the world by the Lord Jesus Christ Himself, there are reports of wars and rumors of wars, famines, pestilences, and earthquakes in many places. But, Jesus of Nazareth said, the end is not yet. These are the beginning of sorrows, but the end is not yet. The four activities suggested by the four horses seem to be going on at that same time.

THE VINDICATION OF THE MARTYRS
(Revelation 6:9–7:3)

> And when he had opened the fifth seal, I saw under the altar the souls of them that were slain for the word of God, and for the testimony which they held (6:9).

The revelation in this will, this purpose, this plan of God includes the persecution of those who put their trust in Him. This seems a strange thing. Actually the Scriptures seem to indicate to us that the suffering of mankind came to its climax in the cross of Calvary. That a wicked man should suffer we could almost accept, but when a good man suffers, it seems strange; and when God suffers, that is astonishing. At the time three disciples were with Jesus of Nazareth on the Mount of Transfiguration, they talked with Him concerning His death, which to them apparently was an amazing thing (Mark 9:1-10). Peter wrote of the death of Jesus Christ that it was something the angels desire to look into (1 Peter 1:12). It is the astonishment of heaven that the will of God should include that His own beloved Son suffer unto death.

As far as we are concerned, when we think of suffering we might say, "We deserve it." In the course of human affairs it seems that many innocent people suffer. Yet we do not know whether we should lay blame, since we cannot be clear in our minds who may be at fault. But we can have in mind that Jesus Christ suffered, and we know He was not at fault. He was "a man of sorrows, and acquainted with grief" (Isa. 53:3). Even with our best understanding, the human mind and heart, though conscious of the things of God, still has to wonder about suffering. And if we think that is strange, we may recall the words of Jesus of Nazareth on the cross while He was suffering: "My God, my God, why hast thou forsaken me?" (Mark 15:34). Those were His words. So we should not blame ourselves if we wonder whether there is something hidden in the wisdom of God. Let us for the moment have this in mind: had God wanted to make the universe so there would be no suffering, He could have done it. We can trust Him. We will trust Him to be able to make all our suffering redound to His glory and to our benefit. "All things work together for good to them that love God, to them who are the called according to his purpose" (Rom. 8:28). Paul goes on to ask, Though there is tribulation, anguish, suffering unto death, will those things keep us away from God? He was persuaded that nothing of any sort could keep us from the love of God which is in Christ Jesus our Lord.

Now, here in this book at this point there is opened another seal. This is included in the will of God. Here are seen the souls of men who were slain because they did the will of God.

> And they cried with a loud voice, saying, How long, O Lord, holy and true, dost thou not judge and avenge our blood on them that dwell on the earth? (6:10).

That is what these martyrs wondered. But they called God holy and true. There was no disposition on the part of those saints to accuse God carelessly.

Job, who suffered more than words can describe, refused to curse God. He complained about his lot and wished he were dead, but he never said anything against God. When his wife told him to curse God and die, he turned on her and said she talked like a foolish woman: "Shall we receive good from the Lord and not evil?" (Job 2:9,10). And then he spoke those classic words "The Lord hath given, the Lord hath taken away, blessed be the name of the Lord." That did not mean that Job was at ease: he was suffering. It did not mean Job was contented. He was not content, though he was trusting during his suffering.

In the vision John saw them, the souls of those who had died because they were true. He heard them and they were calling out to God, "How long are you going to let this go on and not avenge us?" But even so, they called God "holy and true," as if to say, "We are trusting, but we do not understand."

> And white robes were given unto every one of them; and it was said unto them, that they should rest yet for a little season, until their fellow-servants also and their brethren, that should be killed as they were, should be fulfilled (6:11).

Their questions were not answered, but white robes were put on them. God gives each of them a white robe and then says, "Be patient. There are some more down there who are going to have to die as you died, before it is all done."

> And I beheld when he had opened the sixth seal, and, lo, there was a great earthquake: and the sun became black as sackcloth of hair, and the moon became as blood; and the stars of heaven fell unto the earth, even as a fig tree casteth her untimely figs, when she is shaken of a mighty wind. And the heaven departed as a scroll when it is rolled together; and every mountain and island were moved out of their places (6:12-14).

What did John see? It was a vision, like a dream. Everything in cataclysmic catastrophe, everything going to pieces.

> And the kings of the earth, and the great men, and the rich men, and the chief captains, and the mighty men, and every bondman, and every free man, hid themselves in the dens and in the rocks of the mountains (6:15).

Notice here that the cataclysm is seen not only in the stars and the mountains and the sea, but also in that the kings of the earth and the great men all hid themselves in the dens and in the rocks of the mountains.

> And said to the mountains and rocks, Fall on us, and hide us from the face of him that sitteth on the throne, and from the wrath of the Lamb: for the great day of his wrath is come; and who shall be able to stand? (6:16-17).

John had a glimpse here of almighty God's moving into this creation of His in judgment. He is going to move in to deal with all His creation as it deserves. When the realization of the full consequences of their wrongdoing comes upon them, all people of all classes and categories will cower before God and wish that "the mountains would fall upon them." This is a scriptural phrase that occurs in Matthew and in Luke when Jesus of Nazareth is speaking about the latter days. It also occurs in the Old Testament in the Book of Isaiah when the prophet foretells that the day of the Lord will come. The day of the Lord will occur when God deals in judgment and brings to pass the consequences of human conduct and behavior. This judgment will be of such a nature as to cause everyone in every station of life to shrink from the face of God.

The sixth seal has to do with natural calamity. In the physical world John feels the whole creation will be shaken to pieces. This also is a scriptural phrase: "I will shake the heavens and the earth" (Isa. 13:13; Joel 3:16; Hag. 2:6,21). And this is what John saw happening.

At this point comes an interlude. The sixth seal has been opened and looked at, and now there is a pause.

> And after these things I saw four angels standing on the four corners of the earth, holding the four winds of the earth, that the wind should not blow on the earth, nor on the sea, nor on any tree (7:1).

The wind is often spoken of in Scripture as the symbol of the wrath of God. The storm and the wind are illustrations of the wrath of God. The four winds, the four corners of the earth, are physically significant as the four points of the compass are to us. This does not mean to say that John thought the earth is square. It is an idiom, a figure of speech. The winds here would be symbolic of God's venting His wrath upon the earth. We could understand this to imply that God is pouring out His judgment on the earth. John sees the angels holding those winds back: God is ready to judge; innocent people are suffering; people who have done wrong are getting away with things. Around us we see the weak being exploited. We see the strong promoting themselves and taking advantage of their circumstances in sickening fashion. And all the time heaven is silent. Even when we look at Calvary, we see that the sun hid its face for three hours and darkness was on the face of the earth.

"And I saw another angel." The word "angel" is understood in terms of a messenger, one performing God's will, one getting God's will done.

> And I saw another angel ascending from the east, having the seal of the living God: and he cried with a loud voice to the four angels, to whom it was given to hurt the earth and the sea, saying, Hurt not the earth, neither the sea, nor the trees, till we have sealed the servants of our God in their foreheads (7:2-3).

Apparently the messengers of God would not let the judgment of God be poured out on this world until they rescued the servants of God. Peter wrote, "The Lord is not slack concerning his promise, as some men count slackness; but is long-suffering to us-ward, not willing that any should perish, but that all should come to repentance" (2 Peter 3:9). We are encouraged to trust God about the time of His coming. We can confidently leave it in God's hands. Christ Jesus died for those souls. God is meekly, patiently, humbly waiting for those souls. On the day that God moves, these four winds will be let loose. They will sweep over the earth, and it will be too late then for anyone to escape the wrath of God.

Chapter 7

✝ ✝ ✝

PRAISE FROM THE SAVED
(Revelation 7:4–8:4)

> And I heard the number of them which were sealed: and there
> were sealed a hundred and forty and four thousand of all the
> tribes of the children of Israel (7:4).

John includes in his narrative at this point a list of twelve
tribes. We learn in Joshua 13 that each of the twelve tribes
was given territory to possess after the conquest of Canaan—
except Levi. Levi was a priest, and priests did not have to
farm. They were not supposed to work in agriculture, hor-
ticulture, or animal husbandry. They were supposed to serve
the Lord and minister in the temple and do all the things
pertaining to the religious life of the people. They were the
ordained preachers of the day. And we ask, "How did they
live?" They lived off the tithe.

The twelve tribes listed here in John's vision include Levi,
but not Dan. Why? No one knows. I know of nothing in
Scripture that would give any idea as to why that was so.
Twelve tribes are listed, but frankly, I do not think these
twelve tribes represent the personnel of those who are in
heaven. I take this to be again the vision aspect. What John
saw was the twelve tribes of Israel, namely, God's people.

Each tribe numbered twelve thousand. We noted before
that the number twelve symbolizes totality on earth. If four is
an earthly figure and three is a divine figure, three times
four—God working on the earth—makes twelve. We may
note there are twelve sons of Jacob, twelve tribes of Israel,
twelve apostles, and so on. Thousand, we have said before, is
a symbolic number that means a vast number. Ten is completeness: ten fingers, ten toes. Ten times ten times ten

makes a thousand, so that is "the completeness of completion," i.e., a thousand. Now, twelve thousand would be the
idea of the whole thing that was in God's mind: twelve
thousand people of each tribe, meaning all who God has in
mind, and not one of them lost. The fact that the numbers are
so uniform—twelve thousand and twelve thousand to twelve
times—seems to imply the symbolic nature of this part of the
vision. Some have the feeling that when 144,000 martyrs have
been completed, history will come to an end.

This seems to be another place where, in interpreting the
Book of Revelation, the reader can get into confusion when
the numbers of the distances in the vision are taken as literal
and he tries to identify them in this world. If the reader takes
those elements in the vision in the sense of being symbols,
truth can be recognized. In the course of this vision, John had
symbols of things coming to his mind. It would seem that
what John sees here is that God will hold back judgment, the
four winds, until His people, all of them, are safe. The twelve
thousand from each tribe represent a vast number out of all
His people who will be brought safely home before He looses
the day of wrath and judgment.

> After this I beheld, and, lo, a great multitude, which no man
> could number, of all nations, and kindreds, and people, and
> tongues, stood before the throne, and before the Lamb,
> clothed with white robes, and palms in their hands (7:9).

This would seem to show that the number of the saved will be
many from everywhere. The 144,000 whom he saw from the
twelve tribes of Israel were a symbol of God's plan and purpose, to hold back the day of judgment and wrath upon this
world until He had completed His redemptive work and
every last one of His own would be brought in. We can thank
the Lord for that! I have the feeling that is how I will be there.
And that is how you will get in. God is going to make even the
wheels of His judgment stand still till we come in. He wants
to save our souls—and the souls of all others who will trust in
Him.

Here, then, is what happened: a great multitude were
brought in. Elsewhere they are called "thousands upon
thousands upon thousands of thousands," but here it says a
great multitude which no man could number, of all nations.

These were not just the twelve tribes; rather, many kindreds and people and tongues stood before the throne and before the Lamb and were clothed with white robes, with palms in their hands—

> And cried with a loud voice, saying, Salvation to our God which sitteth upon the throne, and unto the Lamb. And all the angels stood round about the throne, and about the elders and the four beasts, and fell before the throne on their faces, and worshiped God, saying, Amen: Blessing, and glory, and wisdom, and thanksgiving, and honour, and power, and might, be unto our God for ever and ever. Amen (7:10-12).

What was the occasion for this outburst of doxology, "Praise God from whom all blessings flow?" What was the occasion for that? All heaven would see that God was going to patiently hold back His righteous judgment till He had saved to the uttermost everyone who would come unto Him. Heaven itself would be moved—astonished!—at this marvelous grace of our loving Lord, grace that is greater than all our sins. Paul said we will be displayed in heaven as trophies of His grace, that throughout all the eternal ages there might be known to all creation the manifold wisdom of God in the saving of us, His people (Eph. 2:7; 3:8-11). The salvation of a sinner is heaven's amazing triumph and wonder and astonishment (Luke 15:10). All heaven and all of God's creation, unite in giving honor and praise and glory and might and power and dominion to God and to the Lamb who made it all possible.

> And one of the elders answered, saying unto me, What are these which are arrayed in white robes? and whence came they? And I said unto him, Sir, thou knowest. And he said to me, These are they which came out of great tribulation, and have washed their robes, and made them white in the blood of the Lamb. Therefore are they before the throne of God, and serve him day and night in his temple: and he that sitteth on the throne shall dwell among them. They shall hunger no more, neither thirst any more; neither shall the sun light on them, nor any heat. For the Lamb which is in the midst of the throne shall feed them, and shall lead them unto living fountains of waters: and God shall wipe away all tears from their eyes (7:13-17).

Here is one of the most precious promises in Scripture. John looks and sees this unfolding of God's great plan and will, which His Son, the Lion of Judah, the Lamb, took from His hand, lived out, and, opening the book, brought to pass. John saw there this wonderful precious gem of mercy and kindness and grace for you and for me. The echoing of that doxology resounds throughout heaven and on and on and on. It is the sweetest song that was ever sung, the song of praise to Him who loved us and gave Himself for us, who washed us in His own blood, loosed us from our sins, and has made us a kingdom of priests unto God. That is what John saw.

> And when he had opened the seventh seal, there was silence in heaven about the space of half an hour. And I saw the seven angels which stood before God; and to them were given seven trumpets (8:1-2).

Commentators have offered different interpretations of that silence, but I am inclined to think it conveys the impression of emphasis. I believe there was silence then because John was to be greatly impressed by what would follow.

"And I saw the seven angels." Again this word seven reminds us how the number seven is used over and over again to imply completeness or totality. When we read of the seven spirits before God, we recognize the Holy Spirit in all His fullness. So when we read of these seven angels here, we think of the messengers of God, the servants of God, in all their function.

The fact that there are seven is not just to be numbered out, as if there are only seven such angels. Rather, these seven are the symbolic number implying all, the total agencies of God. In what follows seven different things will appear, as the total working out, the total functioning of God's will.

"And I saw the seven angels which stood before God; and to them were given seven trumpets." Generally the trumpet implies a loud and important announcement of some sort. It is the instrument heralds used to attract attention to make an announcement.

> And another angel came and stood at the altar, having a golden censer; and there was given unto him much incense, that he should offer it with the prayers of all saints upon the golden altar which was before the throne (8:3).

Earlier in the vision, John saw an angel before the throne with a vial or a vessel of incense, which were the prayers of the saints. Here in John's vision at this time, an angel has a censer filled with incense with which he offers up prayers.

> And the smoke of the incense, which came with the prayers of the saints, ascended up before God out of the angel's hand (8:4).

At this point, when John is looking up and seeing this, there is revealed to him constant adoration, praise, and thanksgiving from the people who belong to God. This worshiping of God is sweet to Him. That is what the perfume of the incense implies. This is to be understood with all else that is going on.

We now gain an insight into the way God does things and what God's mind for the world is. We should understand that in it all there is constant praise going up to God from His own people.

Chapters 8 and 9

✝   ✝   ✝

THE WOES OF THE JUDGMENT OF GOD
(Revelation 8:5–9:15)

> And the angel took the censer, and filled it with fire of the altar, and cast it into the earth: and there were voices, and thunderings, and lightnings, and an earthquake (8:5).

It appears that John saw an angel with a censer filled with incense, for offering up the prayers of the saints to God. And the angel emptied it out, giving God all the praise and the perfume of worship. Then the angel took this same vessel in his hand and filled it with fire from the altar and cast it out upon the earth.

This suggests to me that the will of God was now to be given to the world, to be put out upon the earth. This may be God's response to this praying of the saints. The saints had been praying to God, and now God was going to act in the world. God did this by pouring out this fire from the altar. There were voices, thunder, lightning, and an earthquake: this outworking of God's will had a great effect upon the world.

> And the seven angels which had the seven trumpets prepared themselves to sound. The first angel sounded, and there followed hail and fire mingled with blood, and they were cast upon the earth: and the third part of trees was burnt up, and all green grass was burnt up (8:6-7).

John saw in his vision these seven trumpets. When the first trumpet sounded, announcing to the world the will of God, a great blight attacked the whole plant kingdom. One-third of the trees were destroyed due to hail and fire mixed with blood.

And the second angel sounded, and as it were a great mountain burning with fire was cast into the sea: and the third part of the sea became blood; and the third part of the creatures which were in the sea, and had life, died; and the third part of the ships were destroyed (8:8-9).

With the sounding of the second trumpet it is as if some great volcano has burst out and belched forth into the sea with the profoundest disturbance and disaster. One-third of all the living things of marine life are destroyed.

And the third angel sounded, and there fell a great star from heaven, burning as it were a lamp, and it fell upon the third part of the rivers, and upon the fountains of waters; and the name of the star is called Wormwood: and the third part of the waters became wormwood; and many men died of the waters, because they were made bitter (8:10-11).

When the third trumpet sounded there was a great star—a burning star—falling upon all the fresh water on the earth, so that one-third of the water was destroyed.

And the fourth angel sounded, and the third part of the sun was smitten, and the third part of the moon, and third part of the stars; so as the third part of them was darkened, and the day shone not for a third part of it, and the night likewise (8:12).

When the fourth angel sounded, the sun, moon, and stars—all the heavenly bodies—were smitten, and one-third of the light was put out.

Each of these four trumpets involves some kind of disaster resulting from judgment. The four elements mentioned in this chapter—the plants, marine life, the rivers, and the heavenly bodies—represent four aspects of the natural created world. The earth with its plants, the sea with its marine life, the water running upon the earth with the bearing it has upon the men who need it and drink it, and then the light that comes from the heavens from the sun, moon and stars—in other words, the whole of creation—suffer loss. They suffer partial destruction in the will of God. But this is not all. Verse 13 of this chapter introduces something almost like an interlude.

And I beheld, and heard an angel flying through the midst of heaven, saying with a loud voice, Woe, woe, woe, to the inhabiters of the earth by reason of the other voices of the trumpet of the three angels, which are yet to sound! (8:13).

I suppose that some might feel, "Well, I declare, with the four that have already sounded, can it be any worse than that?" But this is just as though the angel went through the midst of the vision and said, "Now you really are going to have trouble." Up until now the trouble had fallen largely upon the inanimate world and lower forms of life. Then there was silence. After that this angel came through and said, "Woe, woe, woe" for the next three trumpets were going to be worse than the first four.

> And the fifth angel sounded, and I saw a star fall from heaven unto the earth: and to him was given the key of the bottomless pit (9:1).

As we follow this closely, we are impressed time and time again with how much like a dream the narrative is. This passage started with a star and now it is being given a key. The change from a star to an angel as a living being is all without explanation.

> And he opened the bottomless pit; and there arose a smoke out of the pit, as the smoke of a great furnace; and the sun and the air were darkened by reason of the smoke of the pit. And there came out of the smoke locusts upon the earth: and unto them was given power, as the scorpions of the earth have power. And it was commanded them that they should not hurt the grass of the earth, neither any green thing, neither any tree; but only those men which have not the seal of God in their foreheads. And to them it was given that they should not kill them, but that they should be tormented five months: and their torment was as the torment of a scorpion, when he striketh a man. And in those days shall men seek death, and shall not find it; and shall desire to die, and death shall flee from them. And the shapes of the locusts were like unto horses prepared unto battle; and on their heads were as it were crowns like gold, and their faces were as the faces of men (9:2-7).

By now the reader of Revelation could well be confused. But there is clearly the impression of something terrible and harmful. We pause there at the seventh verse, which mentions that the locusts' faces were as the faces of men, because we want to catch our breath before we read on.

> And they had hair as the hair of women, and their teeth were as the teeth of lions (9:8).

The whole sight was horrifying, terrifying. But this is not all.

Whatever our conception of the locusts may have been, it will be changed as we read. We may have thought of a locust as a little creature about the size of our little fingers, but as we read we discover it was something much bigger than that here. Perhaps it was no different in John's mind when he began to see a swarm of locusts; but they grew in his conception, in his vision.

> And they had breastplates, as it were breastplates of iron; and the sound of their wings was as the sound of chariots of many horses running to battle. And they had tails like unto scorpions, and there were stings in their tails: and their power was to hurt men five months. And they had a king over them, which is the angel of the bottomless pit, whose name in the Hebrew tongue is Abaddon, but in the Greek tongue hath his name Apollyon. One woe is past (9:9-12).

"One woe is past" indicates that the trumpet blew. The bottomless pit was opened and those creatures came out. They had the power to hurt men. We should notice that they did not hurt anyone with the mark of God in the forehead. But they hurt all the others. They did not kill anyone; they just hurt them, tormented them.

> One woe is past; and, behold, there come two woes more hereafter. And the sixth angel sounded, and I heard a voice from the four horns of the golden altar which is before God, saying to the sixth angel which had the trumpet, Loose the four angels which are bound in the great river Euphrates. And the four angels were loosed, which were prepared for an hour, and a day, and a month, and a year, for to slay the third part of men (9:12-15).

We have noted before that the word "angel" does not describe any specific kind of appearance. An angel is a messenger, a servant of God, someone who does His bidding. And "angel" does not imply any human form of necessity, although an angel may at any time have had a human form. We do not know what form the angels here in John's vision had. They were messengers who had something to say about what would happen on earth.

When the four angels were loosed, the whole earth process was affected. Here we read there were four angels "bound in the great river Euphrates. And the four angels were loosed, which were prepared for an hour, and a day, and a month, and a year, for to slay the third part of men." This seems to say that God had these agents ready. He had them poised ready to act, and at this point God spoke the word and they were turned loose.

MORE WOES OF THE JUDGMENT OF GOD
(Revelation 9:16-21)

> And the number of the army of the horsemen were two hundred thousand thousand; and I heard the number of them (9:16).

The figure in verse 16 expressed a different way is two hundred million. But let us not count this in that fashion. Simply let this word "thousand" imply a vast number. And a thousand thousand would be a vast, vast number, and two hundred thousand thousand would go beyond our imagination. In other words, it was a very vast number of horsemen.

> And thus I saw the horses in the vision, and them that sat on them, having breastplates of fire, and of jacinth, and brimstone: and the heads of the horses were as the heads of lions; and out of their mouths issued fire and smoke and brimstone (9:17).

We should remember that the Book of Revelation is a vision, and we should not think of these as literal pictures, but as symbols. These are creatures: creations of God that are terrifying and powerful and awful.

> By these three was the third part of men killed, by the fire, and by the smoke, and by the brimstone, which issued out of their mouths. For their power is in their mouth, and in their tails: for their tails were like unto serpents, and had heads, and with them they do hurt (9:18-19).

John was to think of a vast, vast number of units of destructive power turned loose in belligerent hostility against men, killing off one-third of them.

> And the rest of the men which were not killed by these plagues yet repented not of the works of their hands, that they should

not worship devils, and idols of gold, and silver, and brass, and
stone, and of wood: which neither can see, nor hear, nor walk
(9:20).

By now the word "plagues" is used. This passage started out
using the word "horsemen," after it began with four "angels."
But these are various descriptions of this one experience and
event.

Neither repented they of their murders, nor of their sorceries,
nor of their fornication, nor of their thefts (9:21).

And so we get the impression, if we have kept the whole
context in mind, that this is what John saw in heaven when
these seals were opened. The seventh seal has just been broken, with seven angels appearing; these angels had trumpets
which announced aspects of this seventh seal. This was the
last of the great things that were opened to view when the
Lamb took the book and opened it. This is the will of God in
this day and time. This is the way in which God handles things
so far as this world is concerned. In the seventh chapter of
Revelation the souls of the saints were crying out to God and
asking Him how long He would put up with things. Do you
remember how they appealed to God? Why did God not take
mercy upon them and spare them? We recall that they were
told to wait a little while until God had finished His business.
That time was drawing near.

In chapter 9 it is revealed that just as surely as in this world
the people of God have been persecuted, so upon this world
will come the judgment of God. That judgment will fall in a
heavy fashion, as set forth by the seven different angels who
have sounded their trumpets. One-third of the plant life of the
world was destroyed, one-third of the marine life was destroyed, one-third of the fresh water supply was destroyed,
and one-third of the heavenly bodies were destroyed. Then
the bottomless pit was opened, and locust-like creatures were
allowed to come out and torment men for five months. After
that came the horses of war and disaster, and again a third of
men were destroyed.

But now John records that the rest of the men did not
change their minds. With all this suffering, the rest of men
did not turn to Him. This should give us pause. Sometimes

people ask, "Don't you think that suffering actually humbles people?" Not everyone. Some may say, "At least suffering purifies people." No, not everyone. It does affect some, but suffering like fire doesn't purify everybody. In the case of some people, suffering only "burns them up." When they have suffering they just get angry. The more they suffer, the angrier and more bitter they become. When things go against them, they fight. They fight down to the very last—and the last thing they would do is to curse God, no matter how much suffering they had endured.

No, suffering does not affect everyone constructively. Suffering affects believing people. Suffering affects believers in Christ because, though deep down in their hearts they do believe in God, yet in their human hearts and minds there may be much foolishness. The suffering that God allows to come, which may be for chastening, has the effect of burning out the dross and refining the gold and the silver that is in the real believer. But if a person is not a true believer, suffering does not do that to him.

In his vision John saw that with all the suffering that came upon the people, some escaped. But the rest of the men, those not killed by these plagues, "yet repented not of the works of their hands, that they should not worship devils, and idols of gold, and silver, and brass, and stone, and of wood: which neither can see, nor hear, nor walk; neither repented they of their murders, nor of their sorceries, nor of their fornication, nor of their thefts." Even then, they did not repent.

Chapters 10, 11, and 12

† † †

TO THE END OF TIME
(Revelation 10:1-7)

> And I saw another mighty angel come down from heaven,
> clothed with a cloud: and a rainbow was upon his head, and his
> face was as it were the sun, and his feet as pillars of fire: and he
> had in his hand a little book open: and he set his right foot upon
> the sea, and his left foot on the earth, and cried with a loud voice,
> as when a lion roareth: and when he had cried, seven thunders
> uttered their voices. And when the seven thunders had uttered
> their voices, I was about to write: and I heard a voice from
> heaven saying unto me, Seal up those things which the seven
> thunders uttered, and write them not (10:1-4).

Let us note that John heard some things about which he never
wrote. Daniel heard some things he never wrote down. He
was told to shut it up, and not to tell it. There is a lot more
truth than we are given to know. Every now and again some
person may see more than anyone else. There will be some of
us who may see things we cannot tell, things that are not for
publication.

This brings to our mind that God reveals only the things
that will be useful. He discloses only truths that He can make
use of in His great work. There is far more true about God
than has ever been revealed; such things are not contrary to
what has been revealed, but they go beyond anything that has
ever been revealed. God has revealed only such things as by
His grace and by His help we might follow.

John was shown and told many things in this Revelation of
Jesus Christ: some he was to write down that we might read,
but some he was never to tell.

> And the angel which I saw stand upon the sea and upon the
> earth lifted up his hand to heaven, and sware by him that liveth

for ever and ever, who created heaven, and the things that
therein are, and the earth, and the things that therein are, and
the sea, and the things which are therein, that there should be
time no longer: but in the days of the voice of the seventh
angel, when he shall begin to sound, the mystery of God
should be finished, as he hath declared to his servants the
prophets (10:5-7).

This angel solemnly raised his voice and made a great announcement: history would come to an end. In our human
way of thinking, it is difficult to conceive of having no time.
But time was created by God. And as He created time, so will
He end it. You may wonder, "I don't see how we could think
of anything without time." You are right: we cannot think it.
But it would still be true. There should be time no longer.
John simply reported that when the seventh angel began to
sound, God's whole program would be completed and would
come to an end right there.

THE TWO WITNESSES
(Revelation 10:8–11:10)

And the voice which I heard from heaven spake unto me again,
and said, Go and take the little book which is open in the hand
of the angel which standeth upon the sea and upon the earth.
And I went unto the angel, and said unto him, Give me the
little book. And he said unto me, Take it, and eat it up; and it
shall make thy belly bitter, but it shall be in thy mouth sweet as
honey. And I took the little book out of the angel's hand, and
ate it up; and it was in my mouth sweet as honey: and as soon as
I had eaten it, my belly was bitter. And he said unto me, Thou
must prophesy again before many peoples, and nations, and
tongues, and kings (10:8-11).

I am not confident that I will be able to give an exhaustive
interpretation of that passage but the impression upon my
mind is something like this: when God reveals His will to us as
believers, oftentimes it fills our consciousness with sweetness.
What a wonderful thing that God would have His way and
God will do His will. But when we come to realize what it
means, it is often bitter, and for this reason: when God has

His way, evildoers are cut off—and there are many evildoers. When God once begins to act to carry out His will, He is no respecter of persons. Some of us, even some we hold dear, will come under His hand. It is one thing to say gladly "Thy will be done," but it is quite another thing to see it with our own eyes and feel the will of God being done.

When we say so glibly, "Thy will be done," we may not realize that it could mean that some person we know, even a relative, will suffer. When we think about the suffering in the world, we should never think of it as something outside the hand of God. As bad as suffering may be, it is much better that it is in the will of God than that it should be outside the will of God. If there were suffering in this world because God could not do anything about it, then we would really be in trouble. We would indeed be lost if God were not watching over us.

God may, in His own wisdom, allow suffering to come to us. But like David of old, when we come to understand our situation, we realize we are better off in God's hands. It is better that the suffering should come the way He would have it than for us to be out of His hands and have suffering come from another quarter. David was to be punished for having numbered his people, because God did not want him to do it. When David went ahead and numbered his people, God gave him his choice of chastening: one option was to have distress fall upon him from natural things; another was to have an enemy come in and devastate the land; the other was to fall into the hands of God. We remember David's choice. David chose far rather to fall into the hands of God and take God's judgment than to fall into the hands of man (2 Sam. 24).

We should not let it shock us when we read in the Book of Revelation this expression of God's will—which this angel came to reveal—that God would wind up the whole of time and bring an end to everything that there is. Our first impression might be that this is a pleasant prospect, since God's way will be done and God is good. But our deeper realization is bitter, because when God has His way, judgment will come upon those who are out of His will. In this instance John was told, "You must prophesy and you must tell people what God is going to do; it will not be a pleasant thing for them."

> And there was given me a reed like unto a rod: and the angel stood, saying, Rise, and measure the temple of God, and the altar, and them that worship therein (11:1).

The language used here—"measure the temple . . . and the altar, and them that worship therein"—raises the question as to how we can use a yardstick to measure people. But we can understand this function: evaluate things, appraise things, estimate things for what they really are. We are to appreciate the things that pertain to the worship of God. We are to appraise the worship of God by His people.

> But the court which is without the temple leave out, and measure it not; for it is given unto the Gentiles: and the holy city shall they tread under foot forty and two months (11:2).

We need not occupy our time measuring the affairs of unbelieving people, because they will be destroyed anyway.

> And I will give power unto my two witnesses, and they shall prophesy a thousand two hundred and threescore days, clothed in sackcloth (11:3).

"I will give power unto my two witnesses." Many times in Scripture and in various ways, two witnesses are mentioned. When Jesus of Nazareth sent out the seventy disciples, He sent them two by two (Luke 10:1). That idea has been expressed over and over again. Here are two witnesses who are to prophesy 1,260 days. On an average of thirty days to the month, this constitutes forty-two months.

> These are the two olive trees, and the two candlesticks standing before the God of the earth (11:4).

The Old Testament prophets wrote of the two olive trees and the two candlesticks, as in Zechariah 4:2-3, 11-14.

> And if any man will hurt them, fire proceedeth out of their mouth, and devoureth their enemies: and if any man will hurt them, he must in this manner be killed. These have power to shut heaven, that it rain not in the days of their prophecy: and have power over waters to turn them to blood, and to smite the earth with all plagues, as often as they will (11:5-6).

"These have power to shut heaven, that it rain not in the days of their prophecy": this reminds us of Elijah. "And have power over waters to turn them to blood, and to smite the earth with all plagues": this reminds us of Moses. Since this whole chapter deals with these two prophets, we do well to pause for a moment to get these two men in focus. Moses' grave was in Mount Nebo, and no man has ever found his grave. There remains some mystery as we read the account in Deuteronomy 34. It is written that Moses went up into Mount Nebo and was never seen again by human beings. It is further written that God disposed of him there. In the New Testament we read that Michael the archangel strove with Satan over the body of Moses. Michael dared not rail at him, but could only say "The Lord rebuke thee" (Jude 9). The very fact that no man ever found his grave leaves some Bible students feeling that it is possible that the body of Moses was not destroyed in the usual way. We know that Elijah's body was not decayed, because he went up into heaven amid fiery chariots and a whirlwind, in full view of Elisha (2 Kings 2:11-12).

It is interesting that these two men, Elijah and Moses, are the two who appeared with Jesus of Nazareth on the Mount of Transfiguration. The record of that amazing incident in the Gospels tells us that Moses and Elijah came to talk to Him (Matt. 17:1-13; Mark 9:2-10). And they talked with Him concerning His death, which would come to pass in Jerusalem. It seems quite possible these are the "two witnesses" whom John heard about in the vision. If that should be the case, it is also interesting that John heard what would happen to them: they would be killed. Some people take note of this because the Bible says it is given unto man once to die, whereas Elijah didn't. And in the case of Moses, we cannot say he did not die, but no man has ever found his grave. Some thus interpret this passage to show that these two witnesses eventually died.

"And when they shall have finished their testimony": they were to preach and witness for 1,260 days, or 3½ years.

> And when they shall have finished their testimony, the beast that ascendeth out of the bottomless pit shall make war against them, and shall overcome them, and kill them. And their dead bodies shall lie in the street of the great city, which spiritually is called Sodom and Egypt, where also our Lord was crucified (11:7-8).

There needs to be no question that this refers to Jerusalem, because that is where Jesus of Nazareth was crucified. Here it is spiritually called Sodom, as it is by various prophets—who also called it Egypt (Isa. 1:9-10; 3:9; Jer. 23:14).

> And they of the people and kindreds and tongues and nations shall see their dead bodies three days and an half, and shall not suffer their dead bodies to be put in graves. And they that dwell upon the earth shall rejoice over them, and make merry, and shall send gifts one to another; because these two prophets tormented them that dwelt on the earth (11:9-10).

These two prophets who minister the Word of God to the people of the earth, and who preach as Moses did and as Elijah did, offend the people with their preaching. When they are dead, the people on earth rejoice.

HEAVEN REMAINS OPEN
(Revelation 11:11-19)

> And after three days and an half the Spirit of life from God entered into them, and they stood upon their feet; and great fear fell upon them which saw them. And they heard a great voice from heaven saying unto them, Come up hither. And they ascended up to heaven in a cloud; and their enemies beheld them. And the same hour was there a great earthquake, and the tenth part of the city fell, and in the earthquake were slain of men seven thousand: and the remnant were affrighted, and gave glory to the God of heaven. The second woe is past; and, behold, the third woe cometh quickly (11:11-14).

All these things were in the sixth angel's trumpet. This is what happened when the power of war was released.

"Behold, the third woe cometh quickly." There were four angels that blew their trumpets, and they affected the natural world: plant life; marine life; the rivers with the fresh water supply; and the stars in heaven. Then came the locusts with their power to torment, but they did not touch the men with the mark of God in the foreheads. After this came war with all that happened with it, and judgment. And now comes the seventh angel.

> And the seventh angel sounded; and there were great voices in heaven, saying, The kingdoms of this world are become the

kingdoms of our Lord, and of his Christ; and he shall reign for ever and ever (11:15).

At this point the focus of attention seems to shift. Until now, with these six angels blowing their trumpets, things have been bad and worse, with calamity and catastrophe and misery, and all this in the judgment of God. But now the seventh angel sounds and in comes the Victor—in comes the Lord Christ. "And he shall reign for ever and ever."

This reminds us again of all that John has been seeing as he looks up into heaven. We should not forget the original scene. In the center of heaven was the throne, on the throne was He that was, and is, and is to come. Beside the throne was the Lamb. It was the Lamb who took the book and opened it; and then these things began to happen of which we have been reading. But heaven is still open; the throne is still there.

> And the four and twenty elders, which sat before God on their seats, fell upon their faces, and worshipped God, saying, We give thee thanks, O Lord God Almighty, which art, and wast, and art to come; because thou hast taken to thee thy great power, and hast reigned. And the nations were angry, and thy wrath is come, and the time of the dead, that they should be judged, and that thou shouldest give reward unto thy servants the prophets, and to the saints, and them that fear thy name, small and great; and shouldest destroy them which destroy the earth. And the temple of God was opened in heaven, and there was seen in his temple the ark of his testament: and there were lightnings, and voices, and thunderings, and an earthquake, and great hail (11:16-19).

THE COMING OF JESUS CHRIST
(Revelation 12:1-17)

> And there appeared a great wonder in heaven; a woman clothed with the sun, and the moon under her feet, and upon her head a crown of twelve stars: and she being with child cried, travailing in birth, and pained to be delivered. And there appeared another wonder in heaven; and behold a great red dragon, having seven heads and ten horns, and seven crowns upon his heads. And his tail drew the third part of the

> stars of heaven, and did cast them to the earth: and the dragon
> stood before the woman which was ready to be delivered, for to
> devour her child as soon as it was born (12:1-4).

We get ready, as we read this, to see the entry of the Lord
Jesus Christ. We will see the Seed of the woman being
ushered in on the scene. As the Seed of the woman is being
ushered in, Satan is there to destroy Him if that were at all
possible.

> And she brought forth a man child, who was to rule all nations
> with a rod of iron: and her child was caught up unto God, and
> to his throne. And the woman fled into the wilderness, where
> she hath a place prepared of God, that they should feed her
> there a thousand two hundred and three-score days (12:5-6).

Satan was unable to touch Him.

> And there was war in heaven: Michael and his angels fought
> against the dragon; and the dragon fought and his angels, and
> prevailed not; neither was their place found any more in
> heaven. And the great dragon was cast out, that old serpent,
> called the Devil, and Satan, which deceiveth the whole world:
> he was cast out into the earth, and his angels were cast out with
> him (12:7-9).

The coming of Jesus Christ, the birth of Jesus Christ into this
world, the incarnation of God in human flesh, marked the
beginning of the destruction of Satan. And Satan now is cast
out of heaven and into the earth.

> And I heard a loud voice saying in heaven, Now is come salva-
> tion, and strength, and the kingdom of our God, and the power
> of his Christ: for the accuser of our brethren is cast down,
> which accused them before our God day and night. And they
> overcame him by the blood of the Lamb, and by the word of
> their testimony; and they loved not their lives unto the death
> (12:10-11).

That is the way victory would be achieved over Satan.

> Therefore rejoice, ye heavens, and ye that dwell in them. Woe
> to the inhabiters of the earth and of the sea! for the devil is
> come down unto you, having great wrath, because he knoweth
> that he hath but a short time. And when the dragon saw that he
> was cast unto the earth, he persecuted the woman which
> brought forth the man child. And to the woman were given two
> wings of a great eagle, that she might fly into the wilderness,
> into her place, where she is nourished for a time, and times,

and half a time, from the face of the serpent. And the serpent cast out of his mouth water as a flood after the woman, that he might cause her to be carried away of the flood. And the earth helped the woman, and the earth opened her mouth, and swallowed up the flood which the dragon cast out of his mouth. And the dragon was wroth with the woman, and went to make war with the remnant of her seed, which keep the commandments of God, and have the testimony of Jesus Christ (12:12-17).

This marvelous scene as described in chapter 12 opens up before our eyes what John sees will happen when, in the providence and the plan of God, judgment has gone out upon all the earth. In the midst of judgment God will remember mercy and send His Son Jesus Christ. When the Son of God moved into this earthly scene in His incarnation, immediately the issue was joined with Satan. Satan tried to destroy Him. When the Son of God came as a baby, Herod tried to have Him killed. Satan tried to destroy Him, but God took care of Him.

In this vision the woman was persecuted, but God took care of her. Then there was war in heaven, in the spiritual realm, with Michael and his angels warring against Satan and his angels. As this war went on, John heard a loud voice: the voice of triumph. This marked the triumph of the believing people, their enemy being cast down. "And they overcame him by the blood of the Lamb, and by the word of their testimony; and they loved not their lives unto the death."

In that final scene, as the woman was being persecuted, Satan went after her to destroy her. As she fled, he spewed out of his mouth a flood as if to drown her, but the earth opened its mouth and swallowed the flood so that she got away.

Things like this can happen in a dream. They can happen in a vision. But they symbolize something. And what they symbolize is that in this terrific conflict going on, God will not be outdone. As vicious and as artful and as cunning as Satan is, almighty God is greater and more able. God has His eye on His Son, and Christ Jesus is going to win. That is what John gave his people to understand as he wrote about this vision.

Chapters 13 and 14

† † †

THE BEAST OUT OF THE SEA
(Revelation 13:1-10)

> And I stood upon the sand of the sea, and saw a beast rise up out
> of the sea, having seven heads and ten horns, and upon his horns
> ten crowns, and upon his heads the name of blasphemy (13:1).

Many hold that what John saw here in this beast out of the sea
represented the Roman Empire. I do not believe this needs to
be limited to the Roman Empire only; I feel it could represent
political power on the face of the earth. In John's time that
would have been Rome. And as far as we are concerned I
think it still has legitimate bearing on our time.

John was on the Isle of Patmos, a prisoner because of
Roman persecution. The church was entering into Roman
persecution in the days of that apostle, late in the first century. John knew about that and here he saw, in the develop-
ment of this scene, a conflict between Satan and Christ, and in
heaven between Satan and Michael the archangel. Satan was
thrown out of heaven. So on earth Satan has power. He pur-
sues the church but he cannot catch it. It gets away from him.
So he persecutes individuals.

While John is looking at that, there is the opening of
another scene. For the most part it is the same thing seen
again in a different way. This beast coming up out of the sea
could easily be seen to the people living in Palestine as Rome
from across the Mediterranean Sea. Rome had come over the
sea in coming to them.

In any case, John saw this beast rising up out of the sea,
seven heads, and again very difficult to destroy; ten horns,
great power; and upon his horns ten crowns, the power authorized. This implies the beast's total power totally au-

106

thorized. Upon his head was the name of blasphemy. At the time of John's writing, it was the custom for the Romans to consider their emperors to be divine. They called their Caesar god. And that is in keeping with the idea that the heads in this vision had the name of blasphemy upon them.

> And the beast which I saw was like unto a leopard, and his feet were as the feet of a bear, and his mouth as the mouth of a lion: and the dragon gave him his power, and his seat, and great authority (13:2).

This description is similar to one in the Book of Daniel, where beasts with destructive powers are featured. "And the dragon gave him his power, and his seat, and great authority." This clearly brings out the idea that Satan gave to this beast power and government and widespread authority. In the New Testament, in various ways, Satan is spoken of as "the prince of this world." There is a strong intimation, especially when we consider human history, that the power nations have, they have in a destructive fashion. It is easy to see that the power that nations gain, they gain in a selfish way. Each nation standing as it does by itself in the world tends to develop an egotism of its own, a selfishness.

Every nation is like this. Each is very sensitive about others. And nations are ready to fight rather than do anything else. They are suspicious of each other. As we think of these things, we can see that not one of them implies the Spirit of the Lord Jesus Christ. The very destructiveness with which they think of each other, and the very selfishness with which they enter into international affairs, the very intent and desire to get everything they possibly can for themselves, the very disposition they have to keep everybody else subject to them and under them if at all possible—these are not the ways of Christ. It is no doubt true that one nation may have this more developed than another nation. And it can be admitted, as far as our Western nations are concerned, that there may be a strong Christian element in some. As far as the United States is concerned, as far as Great Britain and Canada are concerned, as far as Australia is concerned—these are countries that may have a strong Christian element. While political considerations have doubtless moved them, there can be flashes and moments, times when we sense something else

than merely personal, private, selfish interest. Yet I think
scarcely anyone would challenge the general statement that as
far as our political powers are concerned, the prevailing principle in policy is pretty largely to look out for us and ours and
for those who are with us. We may do as nobly as we can, of
course, but we want to be sure to have our way.

Back in the days of Rome, there were no Christian elements at all in government. National political selfishness was
total and the dragon, Satan, would give to this beast his
power, his seat, and great authority.

> And I saw one of his heads as it were wounded to death; and his
> deadly wound was healed: and all the world wondered after the
> beast (13:3).

Bible scholars point out that John lived during the time when
Nero committed suicide. Nero was the great Roman Emperor
who burned the city of Rome, severely persecuted the
Christians, apparently lost his mind, and died in a state of
mental unbalance. Now that suggests to some scholars that
when John saw "one of his heads [one of the emperors]
wounded to death" and the deadly wound healed, this could
mean that even though Nero acted that way, the government
did not fall apart. The next emperor stepped in and went on
with imperial power.

> And they worshipped the dragon which gave power unto the
> beast: and they worshipped the beast, saying, Who is like unto
> the beast? who is able to make war with him? (13:4).

John does not identify who "they" were. We are given no idea
of this. This may be simply a way of saying the dragon was
worshiped and the beast was worshiped. Worship means as-
cribing the highest power, the greatest authority, the greatest
importance to whatever we hold dear. "And they worshipped
the dragon which gave power unto the beast: and they worshipped the beast." This could be the political power of
Rome, which we will say, to be specific, enjoyed the adoration
and adulation of the people who were ready to say, "Who is
like unto the beast? who is able to make war with him?"

> And there was given unto him a mouth speaking great things
> and blasphemies: and power was given unto him to continue
> forty and two months (13:5).

Here is that forty-two months again. The woman was given a place where she should be fed in the wilderness and be hidden out for forty-two months—1,260 days—a limited period of time. Forty-two months is three and one-half years. Three and one-half is half of seven. Seven years would be a complete period of time. Three and one-half is just half the time, not the whole time: it is a limited time. And this is one of the main aspects of any human activity or any earthly career: it is limited. No matter what we read about what anyone is going to do, or anything that is going on, or anything that is going to happen, it will always be limited. It will not be forever. That seems to be the truth brought out here.

> And he opened his mouth in blasphemy against God, to blaspheme his name, and his tabernacle, and them that dwell in heaven (13:6).

This could be like the power of Rome. Rome did these things in the days of John.

> And it was given unto him to make war with the saints, and to overcome them: and power was given him over all kindreds, and tongues, and nations (13:7).

John saw the persecution of believers in Christ going on round about him. He himself was a victim.

> And all that dwell upon the earth shall worship him, whose names are not written in the book of life of the Lamb slain from the foundation of the world (13:8).

Everyone worshiped the power of Rome except the believers in Christ. The believers in Christ whose names were written in the Lamb's book of life did not do this.

> If any man have an ear, let him hear (13:9).

We should note how this statement is brought in at this time. We remember that John was a prisoner writing on the Isle of Patmos. Whatever he wrote would be read by his political guards, and they would try to find out what John was communicating. But in using these figures—the lion, the bear, and the leopard—which are in the Old Testament, and in referring to these heads, horns, and crowns, which are Old Testament ideas, John would have a pretty safe feeling, I believe, that the guards would not know anything about what he had written. The guards would not get the implication of these images that John had. In any case, when John came to the end of his message he wrote, "If any man have an ear, let him hear." This seems to me to say, "If anyone is able to follow me, let him get the truth of what I am saying."

> He that leadeth into captivity shall go into captivity: he that killeth with the sword must be killed with the sword. Here is the patience and the faith of the saints (13:10).

This is a restatement of a general principle that Jesus of Nazareth stated when Peter was going to fight for Him. The Lord said, "Put up again thy sword into his place: for all they that take the sword shall perish with the sword" (Matt. 26:52). John here is apparently simply passing on the truth that he who leads into captivity will himself become a captive. Rome—which had made believers in Christ captives, had made John a captive on the Isle of Patmos, and had persecuted believers in Christ—would go into captivity. He who kills with the sword, the very one who is killing these believers now with the sword, must be killed with the sword.

"Here is the patience and the faith of the saints." I think by this John is saying, "This is what gives the believers quietness and confidence. This is what gives them patience and faith. They know they will be vindicated. They know that the overruling power of Rome is one day going to be put down. And they can bide their time quietly. Rome may kill them off, but Rome will not win because Rome's time is limited."

THE BEAST OUT OF THE EARTH
(Revelation 13:11-18)

> And I beheld another beast coming up out of the earth; and he had two horns like a lamb, and he spake as a dragon (13:11).

Here is the beast out of the earth in contrast with the beast out of the sea. "And he had two horns like a lamb." This is different. The other had ten horns, which is the evidence of almighty power; but this beast comes up with two horns like a lamb. It looks like something peaceful.

But "he spake as a dragon." This also is different. It reminds us to think about the time when Jacob deceived his father Isaac. We recall that when Isaac was blind, he reached out and said that the hands were the hands of Esau, because he felt the hairy skin of the kidskin that was on the hands of Jacob; but the voice was the voice of Jacob—and that is who it was. Paul said, "I know this, that after my departing shall grievous wolves enter in among you, not sparing the flock" (Acts 20:29). Jesus of Nazareth spoke of certain people who were wolves in sheep's clothing (Matt. 7:15). Here is a beast that looks like a lamb but speaks like a dragon.

This scene portends evil, because the beast coming out now is going to look as if it is a follower of the Lamb of God, but it is not. I do not know what John at that time foresaw, nor whether we understand that this indicates, as some think, a national political totalitarian church. But certainly it is characteristic of governments all over the world. There is not a single dictator or military power who does not soon try to set forth a philosophy that will support his position. When Hitler carried on his great political campaign and rose to such great heights, he undertook to restore to the German people the old Teutonic myths. He wanted to give them a religion. He wanted to get away from Christianity if possible, hoping that he could spread his hatred of the Jews even against the Lord Jesus, because Jesus of Nazareth was born of the Jews. There was too much faith in Christ in Germany for him to succeed completely. But with the assistance of his great philosopher-propagandist, Hitler tried to offer to the German people a religion that he claimed was a German religion. It tried to revive the old myths of pagan Germany which prevailed before the gospel of Christ came into the country.

In much the same way, Shintoism was the strong weapon in the days of the Japanese military and imperial power, for it was their religion. Every nation that has ever tried to dominate in the field of power has always used some form of religion as a means of gaining the hearts of the people. This beast came up out of the earth, with two horns like a lamb, but he spoke as a dragon.

> And he exerciseth all the power of the first beast before him, and causeth the earth and them which dwell therein to worship the first beast, whose deadly wound was healed (13:12).

If this is a national religion, and particularly a unit of religious control in administration, it exercises all the power of the nation, all the political power, and leads the people "to worship the first beast." This religious power causes the people to yield to the political power.

> And he doeth great wonders, so that he maketh fire come down from heaven on the earth in the sight of men (13:13).

This religious power does great wonders, actually accomplishing very impressive things.

> And deceiveth them that dwell on the earth by the means of those miracles which he had power to do in the sight of the beast; saying to them that dwell on the earth, that they should make an image to the beast, which had the wound by a sword, and did live. And he had power to give life unto the image of the beast, that the image of the beast should both speak, and cause that as many as would not worship the image of the beast should be killed (13:14-15).

This will be a strange and impressive and powerful manipulation of control in such a way as to dominate all the people and to put pressure on them to fall in line with the dominant power in the country.

> And he causeth all, both small and great, rich and poor, free and bond, to receive a mark in their right hand, or in their foreheads: and that no man might buy or sell, save he that had the mark, or the name of the beast, or the number of his name (13:16-17).

That is a picture of totalitarianism far beyond anything we know today. This is a certain type of collectivistic control wherein political power backed up by religious emphases will control everything in the country to the degree that if some do not agree, they will not have license to buy or sell or trade or do anything.

> Here is wisdom. Let him that hath understanding count the number of the beast: for it is the number of a man; and his number is Six hundred threescore and six (13:18).

Here is the classic reference that states that 666 is the number of man. I am inclined to think that this represents human nature at its ultimate. The number six indicates the best that man can do: six is the number of man. Seven is perfect: man never gets to be perfect. Six hundred and sixty-six is just six, six, six—man, man, man—just that idea all the way through.

In any case, what John saw was the power of the first beast, and then the power of the second beast, and then the image of the beast, which is a representation of the first beast made to control the hearts, the minds, the thoughts, the activity of men. But it is man all the way through. And when we read to the end of chapter 13, we almost feel like saying, "Now that is the end of everything. What can be done now?"

THE SONG OF THE REDEEMED
(Revelation 14:1-5)

> And I looked, and, lo, a Lamb stood on the mount Sion, and with him a hundred forty and four thousand, having his Father's name written in their foreheads (14:1).

We have read before of these 144,000 in the Book of Revelation. Remember who they were? They were the ones who were called out because they believed in the Lamb, 12,000 from each of the twelve tribes. We paid no more attention to the numbers than to take them as a symbol representing the total number of those who were won on earth by the power of God. When we think of four as the number referring to the earth, and three as the number referring to God, three times four—God working on the earth—makes twelve. There were twelve sons of Jacob, twelve tribes of Israel, twelve apostles: all this brings out that idea. Always there is the idea that this is God working out His will among men. If we have a thousand—which is an indefinite number from a symbolic point of view—then when we have twelve thousand we have a large number representing what God is able to do with man. Twelve times twelve thousand—that is, 144,000—is taking in the whole sweep of what God is able to do on earth with man by His grace and by His power.

Thus John saw the Lamb standing now with 144,000 having

his Father's name written in their foreheads. We have been reading of the persecution going on, but now we see the Lamb coming in judgment. The One of whom we have read as the child of the woman is presented here as the Lamb. And this simply means that, as far as Christ is concerned, He is to be felt all the way through. And here it is again just a matter of the symbol of Christ being brought to the foreground. Every time we see the Lamb in this way we think of the Lord Jesus Christ. This Lamb stood on Mount Zion with 144,000 with His Father's name written in their foreheads.

> And I heard a voice from heaven, as the voice of many waters, and as the voice of a great thunder: and I heard the voice of harpers harping with their harps: and they sung as it were a new song before the throne, and before the four beasts, and the elders: and no man could learn that song but the hundred and forty and four thousand, which were redeemed from the earth (14:2-3).

"The voice of many waters" alludes to the first chapter of Revelation. In that vision John had of Christ His voice was as the voice of many waters (1:15). The phrase "before the four beasts and the elders" takes us back to chapter 4, and we are reminded that this whole Book of Revelation is one revelation. All the way through, these four beasts and the twenty-four elders have never been dismissed. They have all been out there singing while all this has been going on. All were in their presence and "no man could learn that song but the hundred and forty and four thousand, which were redeemed from the earth." This song, the song of the redeemed, no one can sing but the people who were redeemed.

> These are they which were not defiled with women; for they are virgins . . . (14:4).

This refers to a certain sincerity and integrity of their heart relationship with God.

> . . . These are they which follow the Lamb whithersoever he goeth . . . (14:4).

That means they obey the Lord their God and the Lord Jesus Christ in everything.

> . . . These were redeemed from among men, being the first fruits unto God and to the Lamb (14:4).

This is the main reason I take the 144,000 to be symbolic of all who are saved by the grace of the Lord Jesus Christ.

> And in their mouth was found no guile: for they are without fault before the throne of God (14:5).

That is exactly the condition of every believer. So right at the time when the power of evil on earth has come out in the form of this beast from the sea, and then this beast from the earth, and then the image that the beast of the earth made from the beast of the sea with their domination over mankind—just when we think that they have finally brought everything under their control—then the Lamb appears. And when the Lamb appears, He has with Him 144,000, namely, all those who have believed in Him. And they are singing a song. It is the song of the redeemed.

THE COMING OF THE SON OF MAN
(Revelation 14:6-20)

> And I saw another angel fly in the midst of heaven, having the everlasting gospel to preach unto them that dwell on the earth, and to every nation, and kindred, and tongue, and people, saying with a loud voice, Fear God, and give glory to him; for the hour of his judgment is come: and worship him that made heaven, and earth, and the sea, and the fountains of waters (14:6-7).

In the face of this mounting domination of the beast of the sea and the beast of the earth, which I take to be human political power and human religious control, comes this messenger from heaven saying, "Fear God, and give glory to him; for the hour of his judgment is come: and worship him."

> And there followed another angel, saying, Babylon is fallen, is fallen, that great city, because she made all nations drink of the wine of the wrath of her fornication (14:8).

Some have the feeling that John is using the name "Babylon" here as the figurative name for Rome. They hold that the early church knew who or what was meant by Babylon. Peter had called Rome the city of Babylon (1 Peter 5:13). "Babylon is fallen, is fallen" suggests that what this angel is saying in effect is that the power of Rome is doomed.

> And the third angel followed them, saying with a loud voice, If any man worship the beast and his image, and receive his mark in his forehead, or in his hand, the same shall drink of the wine of the wrath of God, which is poured out without mixture into the cup of his indignation; and he shall be tormented with fire and brimstone in the presence of the holy angels, and in the presence of the Lamb: and the smoke of their torment ascendeth up for ever and ever: and they have no rest day nor night, who worship the beast and his image, and whosoever receiveth the mark of his name. Here is the patience of the saints: here are they that keep the commandments of God, and the faith of Jesus. And I heard a voice from heaven saying unto me, Write, Blessed are the dead which die in the Lord from henceforth: Yea, saith the Spirit, that they may rest from their labours; and their works do follow them (14:9-13).

As we read this we will hear things and see things we will not be able to trace out. But we will have one idea clearly, that all those people who worshiped the beast and received his mark would have no rest. All those people who died in the Lord would have rest from their labors. That is a fundamental issue.

> Come unto me, all ye that labour and are heavy laden, and I will give you rest (Matt. 11:28).

> There is no peace, saith my God, to the wicked (Isa. 57:21).

There is a way of understanding the whole gospel in a very simple term of rest. Those who come to the Lord and trust in Him shall find peace.

Cain's awful doom was that he would never have any rest. To be a stranger and a vagabond with no home, no friends, no one—never to have anything, never to have any fellowship, to be alone forever—was the judgment upon Cain. This agrees with everything in Scripture along that line. Whatever else we may see in this vision, when John heard these angels crying out as he did, one thing stands out very clearly: God is sending out word to say that all those who fell in line with that political power and that human religious machine and are trusting in man in any of those ways will never have peace. But those who have put their trust in the Lord and died in Him shall find rest and peace.

> And I looked, and behold a white cloud, and upon the cloud one sat like unto the Son of man, having on his head a golden crown, and in his hand a sharp sickle (14:14).

Now the figure of the Lamb shifts, and as John looks up on the white cloud he sees the Son of Man. Jesus of Nazareth, while He was here on earth, told the people, on that day when He stood before Pilate, that they would see the Son of Man coming in the clouds of heaven in great glory. John saw it. "Behold a white cloud, and upon the cloud one sat like unto the Son of man, having on his head a golden crown, and in his hand a sharp sickle."

> And another angel came out of the temple, crying with a loud voice to him that sat on the cloud, Thrust in thy sickle, and reap: for the time is come for thee to reap; for the harvest of the earth is ripe (14:15).

Wheat and tares have grown together, but the harvest time has come (Matt. 13:24-30). The time for separation is here.

> And he that sat on the cloud thrust in his sickle on the earth; and the earth was reaped. And another angel came out of the temple which is in heaven, he also having a sharp sickle. And another angel came out from the altar, which had power over fire; and cried with a loud cry to him that had the sharp sickle, saying, Thrust in thy sharp sickle, and gather the clusters of the vine of the earth; for her grapes are fully ripe. And the angel thrust in his sickle into the earth, and gathered the vine of the earth, and cast it into the great winepress of the wrath of God. And the winepress was trodden without the city, and blood came out of the winepress, even unto the horse bridles, by the space of a thousand and six hundred furlongs (14:16-20).

Here is a vivid, graphic picture of the wind-up of everything. This is the end of things. This does not mean that from chapter 15 on we observe something after the harvest; actually, as we read on in chapter 15, we may see something that takes us back over this whole story again. This is a sort of a review from one point of view of all history of all times. The Seed of the woman was to overcome Satan. Because of that, there was war in heaven. Following that war in heaven, there was a persecution of the saints down here on earth. That persecution of the saints finally took form in the political power, the religious power, and the ecclesiastical power, all of which have persecuted believers in Christ unmercifully. Finally the Lamb comes in judgment, and harvest time is due upon the whole earth. So actually, in the seventh trumpet of John's vision we have a survey of all history at one time.

When we come to chapter 15, we do not enter into a chronology. We are not to understand that there were the seven seals, and then after that the seven trumpets, and then after that the seven thunders, and then these appearances, and then the seven vials or bowls, as if that were something later. It will be easier to grasp the sense here if we think in this way, that John is being shown something to understand about God's will for His believing people on earth. The revelation given to John was given to the church, and the church was going to withstand, regardless of outward appearances.

The things that the seven seals revealed are true. The things that the seven trumpets sounded and warned about are not unlike the seven seals. They are covering the same period of time in a little different way, but the seven thunders mentioned we do not know. These were true all the time the seven seals were happening. These appearances are always active and true; they had always been so.

And now, coming to the seven bowls or seven vials, we see that they are not something extending on after these others, but we see that they are the same thing the seven trumpets announced. They deal with things in a slightly different way.

We might say that in the case of the trumpets, warnings were given of what God would do. But in the case of the seven vials, we have seven bowls full of the wrath of God. When these are poured out on the world, they do not trickle out drop by drop. Rather, the wrath of God is thrown out, whirled out on the world. In one act of God these things will happen.

In the case of the trumpets there was warning that certain trouble would come to the sea, and certain trouble would come to the land, and certain trouble would come to the water, and certain trouble would come to the heavenly bodies. But when these bowls are poured out, everything in the sea is destroyed, everything on earth is destroyed, everything in the waters is destroyed, everything in the sun is destroyed. In other words, the whole creation is ruined, because when we come to these bowls we have the judgment of God in wrath.

Chapter 15

† † †

THE WRATH OF GOD WILL COME
(Revelation 15:1-8)

> And I saw another sign in heaven, great and marvellous, seven
> angels having the seven last plagues; for in them is filled up the
> wrath of God (15:1).

The first sign was given in chapter 12: "And there appeared a
great wonder in heaven; a woman clothed with the sun." Now
there is another sign, another great wonder in heaven. When
these plagues erupt, there will be no more. This sign has to do
with God dealing in finality with people.

We should prepare our hearts and minds for this revelation
by reminding ourselves that here we look at an aspect of the
truth of God that is commonly unmentioned among us. Usually when this aspect of the truth of God is mentioned, we
shudder and withdraw and wish that the preacher wouldn't
mention these things, because deep down in our hearts we do
not want to think they may be true. I am referring to the fact
that God will one day act in wrath and destroy utterly. We are
not ready for that. Our church culture has become so addicted
to the idea of the mildness of the Lord Jesus Christ that
somehow, deep down in our bones, we think a man is telling
the truth when he tells us that the Lord Jesus Christ is so
gentle, meek, and mild that He never will be anything but
nice and sweet to everyone. As beautiful as that may sound, it
is just not true.

Yet I want to emphasize something right away: the broken
and the contrite heart God will not despise. If you come
humbly to the Lord Jesus Christ, you will never know Him
any other way than as a kind, loving, gentle person. I think I
have had occasions to emphasize to you something of the love

119

of God in Jesus Christ, tenderer than a woman's love, gentler than anything we know on earth. The Lord Jesus is wonderful and marvelous in His kindness and in His mercy toward those who put their trust in Him, toward those who have a humble and contrite heart.

But the Scriptures put it just as plainly as word and illustration can make it that God will judge and destroy whatever does not honor the Lord Jesus Christ His Son. There is a day of wrath coming, and God will not change His mind. It is not that God will suddenly lose His patience and somehow "flip His lid," as it were. He will not get angry and do something rash and disappointing to you. No, what God will do when He moves in judgment He had in mind all the time it would be necessary to do. With all the evil that is going on in the world—all the wickedness, all the carelessness, all the neglect, all the cruelty, all the persecution of the innocent and the pure, all the ignoring and neglect of the weak and of the suffering that goes on in this world—coupled with the pride and the arrogance and the indifference and the carelessness and the foolishness of mankind, together with evil in the spiritual world, we would be led into a serious blunder, a bad mistake, if we got the impression that God will allow this to go on into eternity.

The Scriptures present many illustrations of judgment. Do I need to remind you of the potter at his wheel who makes a vessel and, if it does not suit his purpose, breaks it, crushes it, and makes another? What is the meaning of this vision given to Jeremiah about God and Israel? (Jer. 18). I feel like saying almost in the words of the Gospel of Matthew, Shall we think that the people back in the days of the flood were such greater sinners that they deserved destruction, and no one else will ever get it? Do you suppose that the sinners of Sodom and Gomorrah were so much worse than anyone else that they were destroyed, and no one else will ever be destroyed? Jesus of Nazareth said it would be more tolerable on the day of judgment for the people in Sodom and Gomorrah, than it would be for the people who lived in Capernaum and in Chorazin, cities where He had preached (Matt. 11:20-24). The cities of Chorazin and Capernaum were going to be held responsible because they had heard Jesus of Nazareth preach.

What shall we think about cities today that have churches in them where the gospel is preached with an open Bible, when everybody and anybody could have known? What do you suppose God will do about such? If God does what He did to Sodom and Gomorrah and what He did to the world at the time of the flood, the Scriptures are very plain as to what we can expect. Jesus of Nazareth Himself said that they would see the Son of Man coming in the clouds of heaven and in great glory (Matt. 24:30). Paul told the Thessalonians that they would remember he had told them that the Lord Jesus would be returning with ten thousand of His saints "in flaming fire taking vengeance upon them that know not God" (2 Thess. 1:8). This is the testimony of Scripture.

This may not be the time for us to dwell on these truths to any complete and total length, but we can remind ourselves that when we get insight into the total, overall truth of God for time and eternity, we will be brought face to face with a most sobering fact. When the day of wrath comes, God will judge the world in righteousness by that Man whom He has or-dained. "The times of this ignorance God winked at; but now commandeth all men every where to repent" (Acts 17:30). There is a day coming when the opportunity for repentance is past; God will move in the vindication of every innocent, pure, patient, meek, and mild person who has suffered be-cause evil was rampant on the face of the earth. God will vindicate their faith.

In Revelation 6:9-11 John wrote that he had seen, under the altar, the souls of those who had died because of their faith, how they cried to God to ask Him how long He would let this go on until He would vindicate those who put their trust in Him. They were told to be patient just a little while, and then God would act. Here in chapter 15 we have our first look at what God will do.

> And I saw another sign in heaven, great and marvellous, seven angels having the seven last plagues; for in them is filled up the wrath of God. And I saw as it were a sea of glass mingled with fire: and them that had gotten the victory over the beast, and over his image, and over his mark, and over the number of his name, stand on the sea of glass, having the harps of God (15:1-2).

Each of these series—the seven seals, the seven trumpets,

and now these seven bowls—is introduced by a vision of a triumphant, glorious singing multitude praising almighty God.

> And they sing the song of Moses the servant of God, and the song of the Lamb . . . (15:3).

What a wonderful anthem that will be! They will sing the song of Moses, the song sung when the Israelites crossed the Red Sea and were finally out of Egypt; and the song of the Lamb, the song of the deliverance that was effected for us on Calvary's cross:

> . . . Great and marvellous are thy works, Lord God Almighty; just and true are thy ways, thou King of saints (15:3).

God will judge. He will destroy, but there will be praise to Him. There will be nothing unfair. He will do nothing that is not right. "Just and true are thy ways."

> Who shall not fear thee, O Lord, and glorify thy name? for thou only art holy: for all nations shall come and worship before thee; for thy judgments are made manifest. And after that I looked, and, behold, the temple of the tabernacle of the testimony in heaven was opened: and the seven angels came out of the temple, having the seven plagues, clothed in pure and white linen, and having their breasts girded with golden girdles. And one of the four beasts gave unto the seven angels seven golden vials full of the wrath of God, who liveth for ever and ever. And the temple was filled with smoke from the glory of God, and from his power; and no man was able to enter into the temple, till the seven plagues of the seven angels were fulfilled (15:4-8).

"And the temple was filled with smoke from the glory of God." This is like the Shekinah glory that shone out in the early days when the tabernacle was finished (Exod. 40:34-35) and shown out again when the temple was finished in the days of Solomon (2 Chron. 5:13-14)—several times in the course of Old Testament history. At the time that Isaiah stood in the temple and saw the glory of the Lord, the glory was so marvelous that he was not able to look up into it (Isa. 6). So here, "the temple was filled with smoke from the glory of God, and from his power; and no man was able to enter into the temple, till the seven plagues of the seven angels were fulfilled."

There comes a time when God manifests His glory. He has

manifested His glory on earth in grace. He is manifesting His glory now in grace toward us. And through us He will glorify the name of the Lord Jesus Christ to everyone who believes. God will do something with those who do not believe; God will do something with those who disobey Him. And what God will do with those who disobey Him will again glorify Him in His holiness. All will be revealed when the last deed is done, the last word is spoken, and the last event has happened. It will be found that God kept His word, was honorable and just all the way through, and rendered due account to everyone. Those who are saved will find that He was just and righteous in forgiving us because Jesus Christ died for us.

Chapter 16

† † †

THE BEGINNING OF THE END
(Revelation 16:1-14)

> And I heard a great voice out of the temple saying to the seven
> angels, Go your ways, and pour out the vials of the wrath of God
> upon the earth (16:1).

"Pour out the bowls of the wrath of God upon the earth." This
event is not happening in the world now. This is not taking
place the way many of those other things we saw are; The
seven seals we believe are going on in the world today. The
things the seven trumpets warned about are in the world
today. But this is a picture of the wind-up. This is a picture of
what will be when there isn't going to be any more.

> And the first went, and poured out his vial upon the earth; and
> there fell a noisome and grievous sore upon the men which had
> the mark of the beast, and upon them which worshipped his
> image (16:2).

These ungodly men were afflicted with a disease. They did
not die and they did not get well. That is the beginning of the
suffering of hell.

> And the second angel poured out his vial upon the sea; and it
> became as the blood of a dead man: and every living soul died
> in the sea (16:3).

The Old Testament Scriptures use the word "soul" for any
living creature. That word refers to anything that has life. It is
not the same as the soul of man, but it refers to the soul of the
creatures. Every living creature died in the sea.

> And the third angel poured out his vial upon the rivers and
> fountains of waters; and they became blood (16:4).

These statements are short and terse. There is no description of the consequences. Anyone who reads this can know what they are. There is no point in saying how miserable it is to be sick and diseased and hurting with no cure. There is no point in pointing out what will happen beyond saying that when the sea turned to blood every living thing in it died. So when the rivers and fountains of the waters from which people drink turned to blood, all would be misery.

> And I heard the angel of the waters say, Thou art righteous, O Lord, which art, and wast, and shalt be, because thou hast judged thus (16:5).

What happened was a just judgment. There was nothing wrong about it.

> For they have shed the blood of saints and prophets, and thou hast given them blood to drink; for they are worthy (16:6).

The ungodly person will simply get his dues. "Whatsoever a man soweth, that shall he also reap" (Gal. 6:7). We deal this way with each other; we do not hesitate to think it is right for the other fellow. We flinch from the idea that God would treat anyone this way. But do not forget that Paul wrote to the Galatians, "God is not mocked." No one makes a fool of God.

Ungodly persons are worthy of reaping what they have sown. They killed the saints and the prophets. Now they have blood to drink. It is difficult for me as I preach to stand in a pulpit dedicated to the Lord Jesus Christ, in a sanctuary that resounds with the praises of the grace of God Sunday after Sunday, to emphasize what we are talking about now, because the Lamb is not in sight. This is the roaring of the Lion. Grace and mercy are at an end. The longsuffering of God is finished.

God is patient—unbelievably patient—but man cannot make a fool of Him. God is slow to wrath, but there will come a day when His wrath will descend. When that wrath of God comes, He knows what He is doing. There is nothing hesitant about it. There is no apologetic approach to the matter. He knows that the last report has been in. There is no more hope to do anything with these persons. God is anxious that everyone should be saved; He is waiting for all to come (2 Peter 3:9). But when they do not come, the day arrives when God moves; and this is it.

And the fourth angel poured out his vial upon the sun; and
power was given unto him to scorch men with fire. And men
were scorched with great heat, and blasphemed the name of
God, which hath power over these plagues: and they repented
not to give him glory (16:8-9).

Now the sun is so affected and the ordinary atmospheric conditions so disturbed that living in the situation results in men
being blistered because of the solar penetration. They could
not get away from it. We should remember that this is a vision
like a dream. John is not seeing something that will come to
pass in these literal, physical terms, the way in which it is
described here. He is seeing something in a physical formula-
tion that will come to pass in the will of God.

Yet, for that matter, this event might well happen just this
way. Peter wrote that the whole world which exists now is to
be destroyed by fire. He wrote that the heavens will be
melted with fervent heat (2 Peter 3:10-12).

Such things are written in Scripture. I do not doubt that
such things will be, but what John saw was not a photographic
picture. This vision is a symbol of what is going to happen. Yet
the important aspect in it is that when God's wrath affects the
universe in which we live, the result is that the people living
at the time will be afflicted—terribly afflicted. It is worthy of
note that when the men in the vision were afflicted, they
blasphemed God and repented not. This is something that
believers in Christ can hardly imagine.

I suspect that one or another of us has passed through
suffering experiences. I have no doubt that when suffering has
befallen you, you invariably tended to humble yourself before
God and confess anything that you possibly could think was
wrong in your heart before God. You knew that God would
not do you harm. You knew that God would not chasten you
needlessly, and so you humbly submitted yourself to God.
The suffering you experienced inclined you nearer to Him.

But the Scriptures tell us that it is not that way with unbelieving people. And some of us have had experiences of seeing
how some unbelieving people react to suffering. The more
trouble they have, the harder of heart they get. The more
trouble they have, the more bitter they become. The more
trouble they have, the less they go to church, the less they

want to have anything to do with God. When the time of final judgment comes, these people who face destruction will have no inclination to confess wrong. They will blame God for their trouble. These men in the vision blasphemed God and repented not of their deeds.

> And the fifth angel poured out his vial upon the seat of the beast; and his kingdom was full of darkness; and they gnawed their tongues for pain (16:10).

We have suggested that "the seat of the beast" was political power—Rome at that time. Thus the fifth angel poured out his bowl of wrath upon the political situation that John was in, the Roman Empire. "And his kingdom was full of darkness": this means the beast's kingdom, the political power, got into all kind of confusion. "And they gnawed their tongues for pain": because political confusion, social confusion, civil war, and strife upset people, and it is miserable to endure.

> And blasphemed the God of heaven because of their pains and their sores, and repented not of their deeds (16:11).

They began to have trouble—government trouble, political trouble, internal trouble, community trouble, social trouble—and they blamed God for it. "Why did God let this thing happen?" They cried. They had no thought at all of confessing that they had been wrong themselves.

> And the sixth angel poured out his vial upon the great river Euphrates; and the water thereof was dried up, that the way of the kings of the east might be prepared (16:12).

The river Euphrates was the boundary between Palestine and western Mesopotamia and the hordes in the eastern world. Even in John's time, Rome never had been able to extend her empire much beyond the Euphrates. Back there in the hinterland of the world's nations in Persia and over in India and up in China were areas that Rome never conquered. Alexander the Great, we are told, went as far as India and wept because there were no more worlds to conquer. But Rome never got as far as Alexander had gone, and Rome was the nation that at this time was dominant, and she dominated as far as the Euphrates.

The Euphrates River was a boundary line. The difficulty of crossing it was such that those hordes of the people of the East would be stopped at the river. Now, in the judgment of God, as seen in this vision, this natural barrier is eliminated and those hordes are able to sweep in with the resulting war and distress.

> And I saw three unclean spirits like frogs come out of the mouth of the dragon, and out of the mouth of the beast, and out of the mouth of the false prophet (16:13).

Here John sees the dragon, the beast, and the false prophet again. They all still exist, and while John is having this part of the vision, though it is not mentioned, the throne is still there, and around it are the four beasts and the twenty-four elders. Heaven is still there, where John is seeing these things. But now he is being shown, as it were, a screen. Certain things are being flashed out there before him. John sees these three unclean spirits going out of the mouth of the dragon, which is the devil; the mouth of the beast, which we believe to be the political power of the day; and the mouth of the false prophet, which we think is natural religion, the imitation of the true religion. This would be anything that is Satan's own brand of religion.

There may be something more to be said about this before our study of the Book of Revelation is finished. This false prophet is mentioned throughout the Scriptures. For everything that God has promised to do in Christ Jesus, the devil has a substitute that looks just like the real thing but is not the truth: "having a form of godliness but denying the power thereof" (2 Tim. 3:5). These unclean spirits give all the praise to the beast, to the political arrangement, to the social arrangement, to the human arrangement. All this is under the domination of Satan. When Satan offers to give to Jesus of Nazareth the kingdoms of this world (Matt. 4:8-9), it would appear that Satan has his hand in the political affairs of this world. Evidently he is in a position to do something about that.

In any case, these three unclean spirits in Revelation 16:13 are the spirits of devils, as we learn in verse 14.

> For they are the spirits of devils, working miracles, which go forth unto the kings of the earth and of the whole world, to gather them to the battle of that great day of God Almighty. Behold, I come as a thief. Blessed is he that watcheth, and

> keepeth his garments, lest he walk naked, and they see his
> shame. And he gathered them together into a place called in
> the Hebrew tongue Armageddon (16:14-16).

We should note that "unclean" here simply means that in God's sight they are not authorized from Him. They are not obedient to Him. The word in this context does not mean that the appearance is filthy. Satan has become as a shining light (2 Cor. 11:14). Satan is far too smart to look crooked, and he is far too smart to seem filthy. Satan, a study of his ways reveals, is smooth, affable, suave, neat, impressive. When it comes to listening to messages and to representations of this or that idea, let us beware lest we try to evaluate them by their appearance or what they sound like. There has never been a crook yet that could not make his story sound good and credible. And the smarter a crook he is, the smoother his tale is. So we will never recognize Satan from his appearance.

The only possible way in which any of us can ever be safe is to compare what is being said with the Lord Jesus Christ Himself, because God will never let that light dim. When brought into the presence of the Lord Jesus Christ, the tinsel will sparkle; but apart from the light that shines from the face of the Lord Jesus Christ, no human being is wise enough nor smart enough to be able to distinguish and tell which is which.

These three "unclean" spirits were effective and impressive, and they worked miracles. They gathered all the people together, undoubtedly with inspiring messages. The people were coming together with great hopes and expectations of what these leading spirits would do in bringing them together.

THE CLIMACTIC EVENT
(Revelation 16:17-21)

> And the seventh angel poured out his vial into the air; and
> there came a great voice out of the temple of heaven, from the
> throne, saying, It is done (16:17).

We are studying the last book of the Bible. Preceding the

Book of Revelation are sixty-five other books. So all the Bible comes into focus here in Revelation.

When we see something poured out into the air, it may raise the question to us, Who is "the prince of the power of the air"? (Eph. 2:2). No doubt we readily answer, Satan. And right here the issue is joined in its great, final, climactic event between the power of Christ and the power of Satan.

"The seventh angel poured out his bowl into the air; and there came a great voice out of the temple of heaven, from the throne, saying, It is done." This reminds us of the death of Christ on the cross: "It is finished." When Jesus of Nazareth died on Calvary's cross, His last words were "It is done." Just so about sin, it was done. There was never another thing to be done about sin. It only remains that you and I should believe in Him, trust in Him, and confess unto Him.

With reference to judgment, to the wrath of God, there too will come an end. And here it is:

> And there were voices, and thunders, and lightnings; and there was a great earthquake, such as was not since men were upon the earth, so mighty an earthquake, and so great. And the great city was divided into three parts, and the cities of the nations fell: and great Babylon came in remembrance before God, to give unto her the cup of the wine of the fierceness of his wrath (16:18-19).

When we think of "the great city" being divided into three parts, we might think of a vast building, like an auditorium of some sort, with each wall falling out and the roof caving in, to total ruin. John saw how the whole contour of the earth was completely shaken.

> And every island fled away, and the mountains were not found. And there fell upon men a great hail out of heaven, every stone about the weight of a talent: and men blasphemed God because of the plague of the hail; for the plague thereof was exceeding great (16:20-21).

Chapter 17

† † †

THE COMING OF THE HARLOT
(Revelation 17:1-4)

Chapter 17 does not go on from the seventh bowl, the last judgment, the destruction of all things. The revelation to John does not go on beyond that—it reverts. Having described the seven bowls of God's wrath, now John goes back and takes up one aspect of that wrath.

> And there came one of the seven angels which had the seven vials, and talked with me, saying unto me, Come hither; I will show unto thee the judgment of the great whore that sitteth upon many waters: with whom the kings of the earth have committed fornication, and the inhabitants of the earth have been made drunk with the wine of her fornication (17:1-2).

The judgment of this great harlot happened when these bowls were poured out. One of the seven angels wants to draw special attention to it. Who is this harlot? As the record starts out, it appears to be a woman. But it is not a woman; rather, it is a city. In having the appearance of a woman at this point, she is a symbol, but there is no woman by this name in Scriptural record. This is not some queen such as Athaliah or Jezebel: no one like that.

This very inelegant term "harlot"—which we generally consider is not good form to use, though the Bible uses it quite plainly—should not be interpreted in social relationship. This is not talking about physical, social immorality. Often the Bible uses the words "adultery" and "harlotry" when it is speaking prophetically. The reference is primarily spiritual. God calls on His people to belong to Him. When their hearts do not belong to Him, He calls that fornication. God wanted Israel to belong to Him, but when Israel became enamored with the Assyrians, He called the children of Israel harlots, going after the Assyrians. And Hosea took the instance of his unfaithful wife and preached to Israel that the way she dealt with him is the way Israel was dealing with God. And the way he dealt with his unfaithful wife, to the amazement and astonishment of everyone who reads the Old Testament, so God will deal with unfaithful Israel. "I have loved thee with an everlasting love" is what Israel was to know (see Jer. 31:3).

When James uses the word "you adulterers and adulteresses" he is not limiting his comment only to people guilty of marital infidelity. He goes on to say, "Know ye not that the friendship of the world is enmity with God?" (James 4:4). That is what he is talking about. When the human heart becomes enamored with the things of this world, so that a person becomes more interested in what he likes and what he wants than what God likes and what God wants, the heart is unfaithful to God. Then that person is in God's sight untrue, and the Bible uses the language which all the world understands. The Bible has been translated in more than a thousand different languages, and I warrant you that every one of them has a word for this. I warrant you that there isn't any place human beings live on earth that unfaithfulness isn't described, and that language is a concept that is understandable everywhere in the world. That is the picture here in chapter 17.

> So he carried me away in the spirit into the wilderness: and I saw a woman sit upon a scarlet coloured beast, full of names of blasphemy, having seven heads and ten horns (17:3).

Here we are reminded of that beast out of the sea (Rev. 13:1). That picture comes right in here, except this beast was scarlet colored. That great harlot was now sitting on this beast, and the woman was arrayed in purple and scarlet. This is where the concept of "the scarlet woman" came into our English literature. Whenever anyone uses the term "a scarlet woman," we all know what is meant: it is referring to a woman of illicit conduct and disreputable character in the community.

When thinking of "scarlet," however, we need not turn only to English literature. Isaiah wrote, "Though your sins be as scarlet, they shall be as white as snow" (Isa. 1:18). The "scarlet" idea indicates sin.

> And the woman was arrayed in purple and scarlet colour, and decked with gold and precious stones and pearls, having a golden cup in her hand full of abominations and filthiness of her fornication (17:4).

Purple is the color for queens. "Decked with gold and precious stones and pearls" would seem to be the kind of thing that a woman's heart could be interested in, meaning to say that she has the things she wants. "Having a golden cup in her hand full of abominations and filthiness of her fornication" may not sound very tasty to us, but I am sure it seemed tasty to her. This all meant that she was in a position to indulge herself with the things that would please her.

THE HARLOT AND THE BEAST
(Revelation 17:5-16)

> And upon her forehead was a name written, MYSTERY, BABYLON THE GREAT, THE MOTHER OF HARLOTS AND ABOMINATIONS OF THE EARTH (17:5).

The word "mystery" does not hold here the sense of something that never could be found out, but rather something that is peculiar and strange and serious. A mystery is something we do not know because it is hidden. This is the hidden truth of the matter: "Babylon the great, the Mother of Harlots and Abominations of the Earth." We discover before we are through with this chapter who Babylon is.

We should remember that John was writing something that would pass under the supervision of the local "Gestapo"; it would be examined by the local military police. If he had written down in so many plain words what he had in mind, this letter might never have reached the church. The fact is, John had Rome in mind. But he did not use the name "Rome"; he used the word "Babylon," the name of a city which had long since been destroyed. Now, if someone spoke of Babylon, what would a soldier think about that? He would

think that was foolish talk and let it go. But the church knew
who this was. Peter had used the term (1 Peter 5:13).

> And I saw the woman drunken with the blood of the saints, and
> with the blood of the martyrs of Jesus: and when I saw her, I
> wondered with great admiration (17:6).

This is what John saw. He saw this same woman drunken in
the sense that she was satiated with the blood of the saints and
of the martyrs of Jesus. When I first read "I wondered with
great admiration" I put an exclamation point in the margin of
my Bible at that point. But can we know why John "wondered
with great admiration"? He did not wonder in the sense that
he was morally impressed. He wondered and marveled at the
beauty and the majesty and the glory, the amazing achievements of this person who was fundamentally wicked and evil.
This is the way a person can marvel at what pagan people can
accomplish. Many of us look at statues and pictures, and we
listen to the music of people who are just as evil as they can
be. Some of the most amazing accomplishments of human
mind and hand are carried on by people whose character is
utterly unacceptable.

> And the angel said unto me, Wherefore didst thou marvel? I
> will tell thee the mystery of the woman, and of the beast that
> carrieth her, which hath the seven heads and ten horns. The
> beast that thou sawest was, and is not; and shall ascend out of
> the bottomless pit, and go into perdition . . . (17:7-8).

That phrase "was, and is not" occurs three times. It is found
here—early in verse 8—and later on in verse 8 and then in
verse 11 of this chapter. This should be contrasted with the
Lamb "which was and is and is to be": that is always the
expression of the eternal Son of God (see Rev. 1:4). "He was
and is and shall be" is the way the Lamb is described in the
three tenses. But this beast "was and is not" and yet "is," as
we discover at the end of this chapter. This is an emphasis, a
reference to its temporary character. This is not eternal.

> The beast that thou sawest was, and is not; and shall ascend out
> of the bottomless pit, and go into perdition: and they that dwell
> on the earth shall wonder, whose names were not written in
> the book of life from the foundation of the world, when they
> behold the beast that was, and is not, and yet is (17:8).

Persons who are not believers in Christ will be impressed by this beast, when they behold the beast that was and is not, and yet is. Human beings who do not have the grace of God in their hearts can be profoundly impressed by this temporary world, which is limited and destined to destruction.

> And here is the mind which hath wisdom. The seven heads are seven mountains, on which the woman sitteth (17:9).

Here we can learn what John has in mind. "The seven heads are seven mountains, on which the woman sitteth." It is well-known in literature, in history, and by geography that Rome is the city of the seven hills.

> And there are seven kings: five are fallen, and one is, and the other is not yet come; and when he cometh, he must continue a short space. And the beast that was, and is not, even he is the eighth, and is of the seven, and goeth into perdition (17:10-11).

These things sustain this woman, which is to say, they sustain the great empire known as Rome, the political power which was persecuting the church in John's day.

> And the ten horns which thou sawest are ten kings, which have received no kingdom as yet; but receive power as kings one hour with the beast (17:12).

The expression "one hour" is used once in chapter 17, but it is found at least four times in chapter 18. The "one hour" implies to me a short time. I think one hour always gives the idea of its being a short time. These ten kings who had no kingdom yet at the time John was writing were going to receive their power one hour with the beast.

> These have one mind, and shall give their power and strength unto the beast. These shall make war with the Lamb, and the Lamb shall overcome them: for he is Lord of lords, and King of kings: and they that are with him are called, and chosen, and faithful (17:13-14).

This is the beginning of the victory of the Lamb. John writes they will make war with the Lamb, but this is one time they will find out something. They have been able to kill off the saints, and they have been able to persecute the believers, but now they will come up against the Lord. When they come up against the Lord, they will find out that they are not able to overcome Him.

> And he saith unto me, The waters which thou sawest, where
> the whore sitteth, are peoples, and multitudes, and nations,
> and tongues (17:15).

This verse refers back to the first verse in this chapter. John saw that great harlot that sits upon many waters. We reminded ourselves not to think of it too much as a literal picture: it was a vision. When we read about that beast coming up out of the sea, we took it to be a creature coming up out of human associations. And here it is identified as coming out of peoples, multitudes, nations, and tongues. We can take it that these waters are cultural units, society as a whole.

> And the ten horns which thou sawest upon the beast, these
> shall hate the whore, and shall make her desolate and naked,
> and shall eat her flesh, and burn her with fire (17:16).

Those ten kings, mentioned in verse 12, will receive power in one hour with the beast and they will actually turn against this woman. That suggests to me there will be internal warfare, civil warfare, the like of which broke up the Roman Empire. This seems to show ten kings, who would emerge upon the break-up of the Roman Empire into its separate units, making war on Rome as a nation. This actually did occur in history.

Considering the time when John was on Patmos, this seems to be a prediction literally fulfilled. John was given to see that this woman—this city which sits on the seven hills, which he has obscured in cryptic fashion here, and which I think we properly understand to be Rome—this military, governmental, political power of Rome will actually in a political way give strength to ten local governors or kings. They will rise up in civil war against the nation as a whole, as seems to be indicated by this: they hate the harlot, and make her desolate and naked, and eat her flesh, and burn her with fire.

THE FALL OF BABYLON
(Revelation 17:17–18:5)

> For God hath put in their hearts to fulfil his will, and to agree,
> and give their kingdom unto the beast, until the words of God
> shall be fulfilled (17:17).

John saw that the woman rode on the beast, but the beast would turn against the woman. In actual history Rome rode to prominence on political power, but now political power is going to be her death. That happens over and over again in the providence of God. "God hath put in their hearts" of these ten kings to fulfill His will. They fulfill His will by destroying the very one from whom they received their power.

"And to agree, and give their kingdom unto the beast." Remember that the woman was riding on the beast. Rome was a military power and a political power riding on political ambition and desire on the part of the people as a whole.

> And the woman which thou sawest is that great city, which reigneth over the kings of the earth (17:18).

Other believers in Christ reading what John wrote on Patmos knew exactly about whom he was writing. It was to be hoped that the Roman soldiers when they read it for censorship could not make heads or tails of it. Perhaps that is how many of us feel now when we read it. But the truth would be hidden in there. It seems to me if one reads slowly in this section, one cannot help but see what John was seeing. John was suffering bondage, he was in prison, because of the exercise of this political power of this city of Rome. But he was given insight to see that as powerful as Rome was, and with all the tendency that she had to pull people away from God, she would be destroyed because of internal dissension.

Rome, the ruling power in John's time, is not mentioned by name in this book, but it seems to be pretty clear that he was referring to the city of Rome. Yet it may not be only the city of Rome that John had in mind; it is probably the principle in human affairs that made the city of Rome. When John had this revelation, he had an insight into truth, the reality of creation, of man, of life, of the soul of God, of human destiny. He saw into the reality of things. One of the realities of living in this world was something that was represented by Rome in John's day. This is what we commonly would call human political power: the idea of the power that comes when human beings band themselves together in a governing capacity.

This reminds us of what happened in chapter 11 of Genesis. At that time human beings came together and said, "Go to, let us build us a city and . . . make us a name, lest we be scattered" (v. 4). But at the same time, in Genesis 12, came the call of God to Abraham. One single man was to come out and live with God and receive a promise: "I will bless thee, and make thy name great; . . . and in thee shall all families of the earth be blessed" (vv. 2-3). In the Book of Hebrews we read of Abraham that "he looked for a city which hath foundations, whose builder and maker is God" (11:10). And by that much Abraham was different from the people of Babel.

In the case of the city of Babel in the Old Testament, human beings got together and by their own efforts tried to secure life for themselves. They did not succeed. Abraham came out following God, obeying God, and looking for God to secure things. And Abraham succeeded.

Now, in this latter part of Scripture we will see something that John saw. He saw this drive on the part of mankind to organize himself and structure himself into a social unit. He saw that drive come on through to such a degree of completion that the beast which came up out of the sea seemed to control the whole of society. Men could not buy or sell without his consent. Each person had to have his mark if he were going to be able to do anything on the face of the earth. Those who were under the control of the beast tormented everybody else, trying to establish if at all possible a totalitarian control of human activities in the name and interest of human power.

That was the beast that came up out of the sea as reported in chapter 13. That seems to symbolize political power. Seen back there in the days of Babel, and found all the way through in the course of history, this is what Satan offered to Jesus of Nazareth in the temptation. "Bow down to me and I will give you all the kingdoms on the face of the earth." But Christ refused to do it. "Thou shalt worship the Lord thy God and him only shalt thou serve."

We now know that the Lord Jesus Christ is the King of Kings and Lord of all. But between Satan's drive to gain the control of human relationships by tempting man to seek for personal power, and the Lord's drive to secure and to achieve dominion over the earth, there is this long conflict all through scriptural time, all through history, going on to this present day. It is going on right now in the world even though you and

I cannot see it. It is not given to everyone to see that the powers which are active and dominant in the nations of the world are not the powers of the Lord Jesus Christ. And when the power of the Lord Jesus Christ is dominant it is entirely different from political power. In John's time this was illustrated in Rome.

If someone were to say that John is referring to Rome, I would have no special objection to that, but I do not think he was speaking about Rome specifically or only or finally. I think he was speaking about this political principle that is rampant on the face of the earth. It does not show up only in government; it shows up in business, in great corporations; it shows up in local communities, in domineering people; it shows up in families when we try to get ourselves together so that "me and my wife, my son John, his wife, us four and no more" are the whole business. It is human to strive to make a little closed corporation that will run everything, run all the other people we can lay our hands on. This is that drive to dominate, wherever there are human beings.

In chapter 18 there is a continuation of the same thing, only it is a repetition of it. In chapter 17 the central figure is a woman; in chapter 18 it is a city. But both mean the same thing: it is Babylon. This is not the Babylon on the banks of the Tigris-Euphrates rivers in Mesopotamia, where the original historical Babylon was. This is Rome, obviously sitting on the seven mountains and called Babylon because that was the great name for the capital city of the day.

Chapter 18 is a prediction of the fall of Rome. While we are looking at this and noting how he sees the fall of Rome, we may feel that John saw more than that. John saw the ultimate fall of political power in the whole world.

> And after these things I saw another angel come down from heaven, having great power; and the earth was lightened with his glory. And he cried mightily with a strong voice, saying, Babylon the great is fallen, is fallen, and is become the habitation of devils, and the hold of every foul spirit, and a cage of every unclean and hateful bird. For all nations have drunk of the wine of the wrath of her fornication, and the kings of the earth have committed fornication with her, and the merchants of the earth are waxed rich through the abundance of her delicacies (18:1-3).

All this is figurative language, but it implies that Babylon the great has come to ruin. In the context of the remarks I have been making, this is as much as to say John sees all human aim and drive at security through power come to ruin. When man is thus frustrated in his attempt to achieve security through power, every evil thing will occur in him.

> And I heard another voice from heaven, saying, Come out of her, my people, that ye be not partakers of her sins, and that ye receive not of her plagues (18:4).

This is a call from God to His people to put off being involved in this drive for establishing oneself through violent power. This reminds us of a text in the Old Testament: "Seekest thou great things for thyself? seek them not . . ." (Jer. 45:5). You know how God calls His people, His believing people? "Come out from that." If that principle were put in the terms of the gospel in the words of the Lord Jesus Christ, we would hear "Deny yourself, take up your cross and follow me" (see Matt. 16:24). That is this very principle. That is the call that goes out to God's people. They should not be enmeshed in these human earthly schemes for trying to get satisfaction by human personal effort and dominance over other people.

> For her sins have reached unto heaven, and God hath remembered her iniquities (18:5).

The drive for personal aggrandizement or personal indulgence—the drive to make something out of me out there or in here in any way—leads me into sin. That sin reaches up into high heaven "and God hath remembered her iniquities."

Chapter 18

† † †

THE DESTRUCTION OF THE WICKED
(Revelation 18:6-24)

> Reward her even as she rewarded you, and double unto her
> double according to her works: in the cup which she hath filled
> fill to her double. How much she hath glorified herself, and lived
> deliciously, so much torment and sorrow give her: for she saith
> in her heart, I sit a queen, and am no widow, and shall see no
> sorrow (18:6-7).

The feminine pronoun is used in this passage because it refers
to the city of Babylon, and in the previous chapter it refers to
"that great harlot," and in the chapters before that it referred
to that "beast." It is customary to refer to a city in the
feminine gender. When we speak of the city we say, "She is
like this; she is like that."

But verse 7 of this chapter is a solemn verse: we could
virtually insert our own names. I hate to think of how directly
this would speak to me if I were just to put myself in there:
"How much she hath glorified herself, and lived deliciously."
Lived, that is to say, in a way that pleased me.

"So much torment and sorrow give her: for she saith in her
heart, I sit a queen, and am no widow, and shall see no
sorrow." This is a figurative and dramatic way of giving an
expression to the bumptiousness of the human spirit. This is
how I feel when everything is coming my way, when I think
everything is on my side. This is truly a snare.

> And the kings of the earth, who have committed fornication
> and lived deliciously with her, shall bewail her, and lament for
> her, when they shall see the smoke of her burning, standing

141

afar off for the fear of her torment, saying, Alas, alas, that great
city Babylon, that mighty city! for in one hour is thy judgment
come (18:9-10).

So the kings of the earth—these other powers on earth that
had collaborated with the greatest power—pull out when her
ruin comes. The very people in the world who are your
friends today will be distant tomorrow, if tomorrow brings us
trouble. When trouble comes, they will pull out. These kings
pulled out, stood at a great distance, and lamented: "Ah, too
bad! Too bad! All is over!"

And the merchants of the earth shall weep and mourn over her;
for no man buyeth their merchandise any more: the merchandise of gold, and silver, and precious stones, and of pearls, and
fine linen, and purple, and silk, and scarlet, and all thyine
wood, and all manner vessels of ivory, and all manner vessels of
most precious wood, and of brass, and iron, and marble, and
cinnamon, and odours, and ointments, and frankincense, and
wine, and oil, and fine flour, and wheat, and beasts, and sheep,
and horses, and chariots, and slaves, and souls of men
(18:11-13).

What John saw was like a department store. Babylon had
everything she wanted.

And the fruits that thy soul lusted after are departed from thee,
and all things which were dainty and goodly are departed from
thee, and thou shalt find them no more at all. The merchants of
these things, which were made rich by her, shall stand afar off
for the fear of her torment, weeping and wailing, and saying,
Alas, alas, that great city, that was clothed in fine linen, and
purple, and scarlet, and decked with gold, and precious stones,
and pearls! For in one hour so great riches is come to
nought . . . (18:14-17).

When the time of that judgment comes, the very people who
collaborated in the drive for self-advancement, who contrib-
uted to it and made money out of it, will withdraw. They will
pull out and leave. They will lament, "Too bad, too bad, all
gone, all in a moment."

. . . For in one hour so great riches is come to nought. And
every shipmaster, and all the company in ships, and sailors,
and as many as trade by sea, stood afar off, and cried when they
saw the smoke of her burning, saying, What city is like unto
this great city! And they cast dust on their heads, and cried,
weeping and wailing, saying, Alas, alas that great city, wherein

were made rich all that had ships in the sea by reason of her costliness! for in one hour is she made desolate (18:17-19).

The very people—the kings and the merchants and the sailors—who had profited by Babylon's exploitations and had gone along with her, withdrew and forsook her when the day of her judgment came.

The picture is one of desolation, of being forsaken. This is in the Book of Revelation. In the Book of Genesis it was Cain, who was to be a stranger and a wanderer on the face of the earth. Just as Cain went out without a friend, so Babylon fell without a friend. That is one of the fates of the wicked, to be alone. No one cares. The very people who run with the wicked in the riot of their excess forsake them when the trouble comes.

What an amazing contrast that you and I know about! One thing is true about the Lord Jesus Christ: "I will never leave thee, nor forsake thee" (Heb. 13:5). These are the precious words from the Lord Jesus Christ. We who have committed ourselves to God have the most wonderful thing; we have a Friend "that sticketh closer than a brother." Nowhere in Scripture do we find that any man of God ever died alone. The Lord was with him in that day. What a marvelous comfort we have; but by contrast, what a sad, tragic, desolate outlook it is for us, when we go on our own. In the big or the little, in the deep or the shallow, as the case may be, this principle that John saw here referring to that particular nation is a principle that is as long and as broad as human life on the face of the earth. In every smallest, minute instance as far as we are concerned, these principles will follow.

> Rejoice over her, thou heaven, and ye holy apostles and prophets; for God hath avenged you on her (18:20).

"Rejoice over her"—that is, over this collapsed fallen city of man. Here the Spirit through John is calling on believers in Christ to rejoice in the destruction of earthly power and all that is involved.

> And a mighty angel took up a stone like a great millstone, and cast it into the sea, saying, Thus with violence shall that great city Babylon be thrown down, and shall be found no more at all. And the voice of harpers, and musicians, and of pipers, and trumpeters, shall be heard no more at all in thee; and no

craftsman, of whatsoever craft he be, shall be found any more
in thee; and the sound of a millstone shall be heard no more at
all in thee; and the light of a candle shall shine no more at all in
thee; and the voice of the bridegroom and of the bride shall be
heard no more at all in thee: for thy merchants were the great
men of the earth; for by thy sorceries were all nations deceived.
And in her was found the blood of prophets, and of saints, and
of all that were slain upon the earth (18:21-24).

This passage is just an awful prediction of the total devastation
that would come upon this earthly unit, this thing that was
called Babylon—this thing that was Rome, this thing that is
human effort and human power all the way through. There
will be no more at all. There will be total destruction.

"Rejoice over her, thou heaven, and ye holy apostles and
prophets; for God hath avenged you on her." This note is
struck at various points in Scripture: when God calls upon His
people to rejoice in the destruction of the wicked. Some
psalms are technically called the "Imprecatory Psalms." Some
psalmists prayed that God should destroy the enemy—Psalm
109, for example. I feel sorry that I have heard good and well
meaning people strain themselves and, I am afraid, twist the
Scriptures, trying to say that these psalms are not godly.

Do you feel we should set our minds in a certain kind of
outlook which means that we would never see anything destroyed? What would we do about the Flood? Some will say,
"That was in the Old Testament." What about the cities of
Sodom and Gomorrah? That also is in the Old Testament.
When we mention the word "hell," some will only shudder.
Such people seem to be willingly ignorant of the fact that the
one person who taught more about hell in the Bible than
anyone else is the Lord Jesus Christ.

If in your heart you have some appreciation of God, has it
occurred to you how He has been insulted by human beings?
Has it occurred to you how God has been dealt with by people
who take every good thing from Him, please themselves as
they see fit, yet never give Him any praise? Such persons use
His name only in blasphemy. They blame Him for everything
that is bad, while they take all the credit for themselves for
everything that is good. Some hurt the innocent or the poor
and take advantage of everyone that they possibly can. Such
live in this world just as they please, while God in heaven is

grieved with everything that He sees. Can you realize that, or can you feel it in your spirit? When we are conscious of these things, the Holy Spirit enables us to realize that destruction from His presence is the proper fate of these people.

"Our God is a consuming fire" is New Testament language (Heb. 12:29). When our hearts would really honor God, we would be filled with an emotion to see God glorified. We cannot possibly tolerate anything that grieves Him who loved us and gave Himself for us. Patient, longsuffering, holy, righteous, just, good is this almighty God who is defied and despised and shamed by these creatures on earth. Even that is not the worst thing: they harm the innocent and the poor and they shut out from heaven those who would come into heaven if they would leave them alone. Do you think that God should stand by and let such things happen?

We need to remind ourselves of Paul's statement: "Be not deceived; God is not mocked" (Gal. 6:7). When we come to the point where our hearts and spirits are totally given over to God and we consider what God has done, He will lift us from within. When I say "Rejoice" it is not quite like saying "Be glad." "Rejoice" is to have the inward satisfaction, a real abiding total satisfaction in the idea that the name of God will be vindicated and God will be glorified. Whatever is displeasing and shaming to Him will be destroyed. And the Holy Spirit can bring us to where we will agree with Him on that.

It is the people who know they are lost that appreciate a Savior. "Knowing therefore the terror of the Lord, we [seek to] persuade men" (2 Cor. 5:11). The greatest dynamic, the greatest urge that puts people into working in Sunday school and youth work trying to win children and young people to God, are the people who believe that the soul that is lost will be destroyed. Wherever you see Sunday schools promoted they are promoted by people who really believe that by teaching the gospel, they are saving souls. They seek to save souls that would be lost if the gospel were not taken to them.

It actually robs us of the disposition to sacrifice if we get this superficial erroneous notion that everything is going to be all right with God. To feel that "everything goes" is simply not true! Sobering as this fact may be, it is definitely not true. There is only one way for you and I to be able to stand in the presence of God, and that is through believing in the Lord Jesus Christ. If someone were to say, "I just do not understand God's doing that," I could say to that person very sympathetically, I don't wonder at that. One of the difficulties in understanding that person is that at the best all he has is a human heart. God is God, and you and I are just human beings. We will just have to leave some things with God that you and I do not know.

But if anyone wonders about God's being gracious and merciful: there is one thing he should do: he should look into the face of Jesus Christ. He should continue looking into His face, and while he is looking into His face he should remember one thing: Christ Jesus came as Savior. Jesus Christ is in this same world as Savior now. His hands are outstretched and He is saying, "Come unto me, all ye that labour and are heavy laden, and I will give you rest" (Matt. 11:28). And even that is not all that is true about the Lord Jesus Christ. In Revelation 19 and 20 we shall find that Christ is coming in all the power that God has given Him to establish God's kingdom in the universe. In so doing Christ completely removes the things that are evil. It will take violence to do it, and He is going to be violent at that point. He will rule the nations with a rod of iron.

Chapters 19 and 20

† † †

THE HALLELUJAH CHORUS
(Revelation 19:1-7)

We read in chapter 18 of a spirit of great joy over the destruction of the wicked city. The theme changes in chapter 19.

> And after these things I heard a great voice of much people in heaven, saying, Alleluia; Salvation, and glory, and honour, and power, unto the Lord our God: for true and righteous are his judgments; for he hath judged the great whore, which did corrupt the earth with her fornication, and hath avenged the blood of his servants at her hand (19:1-2).

The shout "Alleluia; Salvation, and glory, and honour, and power, unto the Lord our God" went up from a great multitude. "I heard a great voice of much people in heaven." They were singing the praise of God because He had vindicated the faith of those who put their trust in Him. God will not be able to vindicate the faith of those who put their trust in Him, apart from destroying those who abused and persecuted His people here on the face of the earth.

Consider some person, living in a family situation, whose heart has been touched by the grace of God, who knows what the will of God is for her, so that she spends her days serving, humbly doing. She may not even be able to come to church except on rare occasions, because she has so much work to do. She may not be able to give more than a pittance to missions because she is not even allowed to handle money. Working, serving, abused, neglected, taken advantage of, imposed upon, suffering in any number of ways, she eventually dies in such a state. Never once did she have anything that would count as a fair break as far as this world is concerned. Now is that to fall discarded and forgotten as "just one of those things"? Shall we say it is "just too bad"?

There is a God in heaven who heard every cry, felt every sigh, was touched with every feeling of infirmity of that faithful servant of His, that handmaiden of His. What times that woman in her own quiet way trusted her almighty Father in heaven, what times His Spirit comforted her, nobody knew. So she lived on through. I do not doubt that even perhaps in this world she may have received many a favor in blessedness in her own soul because of the fellowship she had with her living Lord. But should we think that is all there is to it? Don't you think that when the time comes, all things will be open before the eyes of Him with whom we have to do? That He will set this matter straight in a way that will glorify Him? I would not say He will pay back and retaliate, because I am satisfied this woman would not want that kind of thing. But when all is said and done, she will be glorified.

Consider the parable of the rich man and Lazarus (Luke 16). There this whole matter is pictured for us by the Lord Himself. Lazarus was a beggar. He never had anything in this world. The rich man had everything with pomp and comfort. Jesus of Nazareth told the story, how that when they died, the poor man went to heaven and the rich man went to hell, in torment. This kind of thing is to be seen over and over again in Scripture. Here in Revelation 19 God is praised because He has vindicated the faith of those who trust in Him.

What human being on earth has any understanding or even any consciousness of the misery and the suffering that the martyrs have endured all the way from the beginning of time down to recent days? People have been put to death because they believed. There have been people whose bodies were not killed, but whose spirits were burdened and abused.

> And again they said, Alleluia. And her smoke rose up for ever and ever (19:3).

This must be the smoke of the city of Babylon. There is praise to God for His righteous judgment, for completely destroying that among men which had built itself up in self-indulgence to the hurt of the innocent and the poor and the weak.

> And the four and twenty elders and the four beasts fell down
> and worshipped God that sat on the throne, saying, Amen;
> Alleluia (19:4).

Remember that all the time during John's vision, in the center
of heaven was the throne. And on the throne sat God. This
must always be one of the very central aspects of our whole
understanding: on the throne is God. And these four beasts
and twenty-four elders fell down and worshiped God, saying,
"Amen; Alleluia." All through Scripture "Amen" is an exclamation that you and I use to this day which is to say "Even so,
Lord. Let it be so."

> And a voice came out of the throne, saying, Praise our God, all
> ye his servants, and ye that fear him, both small and great. And
> I heard as it were the voice of a great multitude, and as the
> voice of many waters, and as the voice of mighty thunderings,
> saying, Alleluia: for the Lord God omnipotent reigneth. Let us
> be glad and rejoice, and give honour to him: for the marriage of
> the Lamb is come, and his wife hath made herself ready
> (19:5-7).

What a revelation this would have been back in that day when
John was a prisoner on the isle of Patmos, and the early
church was being persecuted bitterly by the pagan Romans
who undertook to stamp them out and to kill them all unless
they would worship their emperor! What a stirring challenge
John sent out when he wrote, "I saw and I heard!" In heaven
they were all praising God because He is omnipotent, almighty; and He reigns forever and ever. Believers in Christ
can take courage. Even if they never in this world get one
single bit of consideration, they are safe in Him who keeps all
things in His hands.

This is the only place in the New Testament that the word
"Alleluia" occurs. This is the origin of the great Hallelujah
Chorus which some of the world's greatest musicians have
tried to put to music. This is the inspiration for the idea. The
great Hallelujah Chorus will be sung in heaven. And that
Hallelujah Chorus will ring out at a time when it becomes
obvious that God is going to manifest His sovereign control by
lifting up that which is righteous in His sight, and destroying
that which is unrighteous in His sight.

THE COMING OF THE KING OF KINGS
(Revelation 19:8-16)

> And to her was granted that she should be arrayed in fine linen,
> clean and white: for the fine linen is the righteousness of saints.
> And he saith unto me, Write, Blessed are they which are called
> unto the marriage supper of the Lamb. And he saith unto me,
> These are the true sayings of God (19:8-9).

This vision of John's did not appear to be a historical event,
because it is unclear what John sees as the role of the saints.
The marriage supper of the Lamb will include all believers in
Christ. In verses 7 and 8 the saints are included in the bride,
the wife of the Lamb; whereas in verse 9 they are included in
the guests. The shifting of the figure is just the way John saw it
in the vision. And now we come to verse 10, and I want to
draw your attention to something here that to my mind is very
striking. You will find nothing else quite like this anywhere in
the New Testament.

> And I fell at his feet to worship him. And he said unto me, See
> thou do it not: I am thy fellowservant, and of thy brethren that
> have the testimony of Jesus: worship God: for the testimony of
> Jesus is the spirit of prophecy (19:10).

What was John prompted to do? Here is an angel who brought
him this insight, this marvelous, lifting, encouraging, wonderful outlook: God will rule, and God will vindicate those
who put their trust in Him. John is so moved he wants to bow
down and reverence this messenger. But the messenger says,
"Don't do it. Don't treat me like that. I am just like you are.
We are all brethren who have the testimony of Jesus. We
have our personal tribute to give to the Son of God."

What really activates a message from God, an honest and
true message from God, will come in the name of Jesus
Christ. Anytime we listen to any kind of representation or any
program or any proposition that does not feature and put in
the very center the Lord Jesus Christ and His works, past,
present, and future; when anyone offers a solution to any
human situation and does not have that solution occur because the living Lord in heaven is interceding on our behalf;
when anyone would think to see any kind of solution of an
earthly problem apart from the Lord Jesus Christ Himself,
King of Kings and Lord of Lords—mark down that it is not

true. It is just not true to the fact. God has given all government into the hand of His Son: "All power in heaven and on
earth is given unto me." The Lord Jesus Christ is the only
begotten Son of God. "I am the way, the truth, and the life: no
man cometh unto the Father, but by me" (John 14:6). "I am
the door: by me if any man enter in, he shall be saved, and
shall go in and out, and find pasture" (John 10:9). Anyone who
seeks to enter any other way is a thief and a robber.

When I was studying this passage, I was stopped in my
tracks to notice the words at the end of verse 9: "These are the
true sayings of God." We have to say that our teaching, our
preaching, our praying, our thinking, our hoping must be in
the name of the Lord Jesus Christ.

Why should we who believe in Christ ever lose our contact
with Him who loved us and gave Himself for us? Is there any
one of us who supposes we could stand in the presence of
God, apart from the Lord Jesus Christ? Does anyone for one
moment think he can enter into heaven apart from the Lord
Jesus Christ? Then let us be candid, and let us be intelligent
about this matter; let us keep our attention focused upon
Him. The first move the enemy would make is to get our eyes
fixed on something else than the Lord Jesus Christ. An easy
thing to focus people's attention upon is human nature. But
almighty God has decreed that at the name of Jesus every
knee shall bow, every tongue confess that He is Christ, to the
glory of God the Father (see Rom. 14:11).

> And I saw heaven opened, and behold a white horse; and he
> that sat upon him was called Faithful and True, and in right-
> eousness he doth judge and make war (19:11).

We will now see the Lord Jesus Christ. He will come, but He
is not coming as a Lamb. He is not coming as the Babe of
Bethlehem. He is coming as a warrior on a charger. He is
riding this white horse, which back in the days of John was an
instrument to battle. The scene would not be pictured this
way today. If Christ were to ride a jet bomber, it would be
fitting for today. But John saw Him coming on a white horse.

"And he that sat upon him was called Faithful and True,
and in righteousness he doth judge and make war." This is
something different from what we have ever heard about the

Lord Jesus Christ. He came in gentleness and mildness, in meekness and in peace, calling people winsomely, inviting them with kindness to come unto Him. But we need to remember that the bowl, the vial of God's wrath, had been poured out. We are about to see here the wind-up of the whole business. In this conclusion to the whole creation, God will put into the hands of Him, whom the world rejected and killed, the power to make all nations, all creation, bow before His will. If this sounds hard, it is not nearly so hard as it will be. If anyone should think, "I don't see how that can be," he should ask himself where he gets his ideas. If anyone should wonder that anything like this could happen, he should consider what has happened in this world in the last twenty-five years. Does one think trouble could not come? Can he think disaster could not strike? Can he think destruction could not occur? Can one think that if men could blow a city off the map with a bomb, it is impossible for God to do something? If destruction is a weapon of man, why should not God employ it? He will. "In righteousness he doth judge and make war."

> His eyes were as a flame of fire, and on his head were many crowns; and he had a name written, that no man knew, but he himself (19:12).

This is symbolic again. This is the King of Kings. He bears in Himself all authority. Four names of the Lord Jesus Christ are referred to in this chapter. The first one is "Faithful and True." The second one is not written—as verse 12 indicates. The second name He has for Himself. What God calls Him is not revealed to us.

> And he was clothed with a vesture dipped in blood: and his name is called The Word of God (19:13).

We recall that "In the beginning was the Word, and the Word was with God, and the Word was God. The same was in the beginning with God" (John 1:1-2). This is the same Word. Now Christ comes as the Word of God, His third name. In other words, the expressed activation of the will of God, the One who actually carries out the will of God, is the Word of God. The will of God expressed is the Word of God, and here the will of God activated in a Person is the Word of God: the Son of God who came to do the Father's will.

> And the armies which were in heaven followed him upon white horses, clothed in fine linen, white and clean. And out of his mouth goeth a sharp sword, that with it he should smite the nations: and he shall rule them with a rod of iron: and he treadeth the winepress of the fierceness and wrath of Almighty God (19:14-15).

This conquest was revealed in Psalm 2. It is revealed all through the Old Testament, and it is mentioned also in the New Testament. But here is the event at last.

> And he hath on his vesture and on his thigh a name written, KING OF KINGS, AND LORD OF LORDS (19:16).

So these are the four names of Christ: Faithful and True; the second one, that no human being, but only God, knows; The Word of God; KING OF KINGS AND LORD OF LORDS.

THE BINDING OF SATAN
(Revelation 19:17–20:10)

> And I saw an angel standing in the sun; and he cried with a loud voice, saying to all the fowls that fly in the midst of heaven, Come and gather yourselves together unto the supper of the great God; that ye may eat the flesh of kings, and the flesh of captains, and the flesh of mighty men, and the flesh of horses, and of them that sit on them, and the flesh of all men, both free and bond, both small and great (19:17-18).

This pictures a tremendous destruction.

> And I saw the beast, and the kings of the earth, and their armies, gathered together to make war against him that sat on the horse, and against his army (19:19).

Remember the beast, the one who came up out of the sea, the one who gave power to the woman, to Babylon?

> And the beast was taken, and with him the false prophet that wrought miracles before him, with which he deceived them that had received the mark of the beast, and them that worshipped his image. These both were cast alive into a lake of fire burning with brimstone (19:20).

This political power and this false human religion—"these both were cast alive into a lake of fire."

> And the remnant were slain with the sword of him that sat
> upon the horse, which sword proceeded out of his mouth: and
> all the fowls were filled with their flesh (19:21).

As we read this description of what John saw, we see first that it seems that the King of Kings has the sword in His hand and then He has the sword in His mouth. We have never seen anything like this. It is a symbolic, picturesque, impressive way of visualizing the truth brought to John's spirit that the Lord Jesus Christ will come in the power of heaven in great glory with His saints, "taking vengeance on them that know not God," as we read in 2 Thessalonians 1:8.

Chapters 17, 18, and 19 are the wind-up of earthly affairs. As we read on in chapter 20 we will see this again. As we look at this we should remember that these things do not necessarily follow each other in chronological order. John sees one picture, then he sees another picture—but that does not mean that the other picture happened after the first picture. It may be that this second picture merely illustrates and magnifies something in the first one. Then John sees another one, and this does not mean that this one came first or last or in the middle—but it came. In other words, each of these successive pictures reveals some aspect of truth.

In chapter 20 we have a continuation of what John saw about the real truth of God in the ultimate.

> And I saw an angel come down from heaven, having the key of
> the bottomless pit and a great chain in his hand (20:1).

Note clearly what John writes, because I am going to emphasize that every descriptive term here is symbolic. Do you know what a pit would be like! A hole like a mine shaft. It would have a lid on it to cover it. It would be a containing place, like a dungeon. The iron chain is a symbol of something: the power to restrain and control.

> And he laid hold on the dragon, that old serpent, which is the
> Devil, and Satan, and bound him a thousand years (20:2).

Perhaps at one time or another some of us may have wondered who the dragon is. And then again, who is the old serpent? Or perhaps, who is the devil? Who is Satan? If we have heard these words used before, we possibly have tried to visualize the dragon. We may have tried to visualize the serpent. We may even have tried to visualize the devil, even though we would not know for sure how to picture him. Then we would have tried to visualize Satan, though we would not know how to picture him. I do not think there were four entities; these are four names of one being. This verse providentially puts them all together.

I have the feeling at times that among believers in Christ we are a long way from an adult realization, a mature conception, of the power of Satan to gain the consent of people to attempt something for personal aggrandizement. No matter whether it involves a nation or a society or a business organization, Satan knows how to do it. He is allowed to tempt people in this way. It is this kind of thing with which the word "dragon" is associated. The word "serpent" is always associated with tempting man to sin, as he did in the days of the Garden of Eden. Wherever we find the word "serpent," there is a wily cunning approach tempting man at his weakest point to somehow step out of line with God.

"The devil" is primarily the accuser of the brethren. Have you ever wondered how easy it is for us to listen avidly to something that hurts some other believer in Christ? Have you ever wondered why we have such itchy ears to hear about something that isn't quite "kosher" in the church. Has it ever dawned on you that we are being tempted to say things that accuse somebody else, who really belongs to us? Do we realize, when we give in, that we are hurting the body of Christ? Do we realize what the Lord Jesus Christ does with the sins of our brethren? He covers them.

Suppose we knew that something wrong happened in our congregation. Do we know what Jesus Christ did? He died for that. And what is more, He repeated the gossip to nobody. Have we any idea what the devil would do? The devil would get on the phone the first chance he had and call up someone to tell what he had heard about somebody in the church. If we do that, we are eating out the heart of the church, and we are hurting the body of Christ. Actually we will be doing the devil's work. You and I can actually serve God by foiling the devil. So do not do his work about accusing the brethren.

Here in Revelation we read that this angel "laid hold on the dragon, that old serpent," and bound him a thousand years,

> And cast him into the bottomless pit, and shut him up, and set a seal upon him, that he should deceive the nations no more, till the thousand years should be fulfilled: and after that he must be loosed a little season. And I saw thrones, and they sat upon them, and judgment was given unto them: and I saw the souls of them that were beheaded for the witness of Jesus, and for the word of God, and which had not worshipped the beast, neither his image, neither had received his mark upon their foreheads, or in their hands; and they lived and reigned with Christ a thousand years. But the rest of the dead lived not again until the thousand years were finished. This is the first resurrection. Blessed and holy is he that hath part in the first resurrection: on such the second death hath no power, but they shall be priests of God and of Christ, and shall reign with him a thousand years. And when the thousand years are expired, Satan shall be loosed out of his prison, and shall go out to deceive the nations which are in the four quarters of the earth, Gog and Magog, to gather them together to battle: the number of whom is as the sand of the sea. And they went up on the breadth of the earth, and compassed the camp of the saints about, and the beloved city: and fire came down from God out of heaven, and devoured them. And the devil that deceived them was cast into the lake of fire and brimstone, where the beast and the false prophet are, and shall be tormented day and night for ever and ever (20:3-10).

This is the last we will hear of the devil in the Book of Revelation. We can put down there "all gone."

I want to proceed slowly through this chapter. I will suggest to you what I think is true here, because in this passage I read all that the Bible has to say about the thousand years. I call this period "a thousand years," because that does not sound so striking as if I said "the millennium." That is the thousand years. And this is all that the Bible says about the thousand years. It is commonly called "the millennium."

A KINGDOM OF PRIESTS
(Revelation 20:3-10)

What is said about the millennium by good men, by Bible students, has filled volumes and volumes and created a lot of controversy. There is, for example, the binding of Satan: when we see this word "binding," this undoubtedly does not mean he was killed. It means he was contained or restrained. He was still alive. We recall that after a thousand years he was loose for "a little season." And he was finally thrown into the lake of fire (v. 10); but not at this time (v. 3).

Now, if any of us have ever handled a vicious dog, we know that when we chained him up, it did not mean we killed him. It has been written—and I read this with some amusement—that if Satan was chained, he was certainly chained on a long tether. Because he seems to get around a great deal.

But let us consider that the meaning of the chain is "restraint." This opens an entirely new idea of the work of Christ in this world. I am beginning to believe that the Lord Jesus Christ did more about the welfare of mankind when He died on Calvary's cross than many of us evangelicals oftentimes realize. Satan is restrained by the preaching of the gospel far more than we commonly recognize. I know that it is true that he goes about "as a roaring lion" seeking whom he may devour, but we know he cannot touch one of God's own without consent. Do we remember that in 1 John we read: ". . . he that is begotten of God keepeth himself, and that wicked one toucheth him not" (1 John 5:18)? Do we know that actually, as far as God's arrangement of things is concerned in the work of Christ, any person humbly trusting in the Lord Jesus Christ is delivered from the ravages of Satan? Satan can tempt us, but he cannot lay hold on us.

A time is coming when God will allow this restrained tendency to call man to flaunt himself and make himself equal with God, to run unchecked. But right now it isn't so. Actually, in the world in which we are living, things are not nearly so bad as they would be if the evil in men's hearts were allowed to run rampant. Despite all the ambitions of evil that we find on the face of the earth, amazingly we have considerable liberty for righteousness. But the very passage that I have just quoted informs us that there will come a time in this world when this liberty will be gone, and evil will be allowed to increase unrestrained.

This principle of diverting the heart of man from any appreciation of God and Jesus Christ, to the point where it would make man into God and to become enamored with human power, will one day be allowed full sway. Satan will again be permitted to tempt man and deceive man into thinking that if man will serve him, man can satisfy himself.

I believe all this is involved with the "binding" that is mentioned here in verses 2 and 3. Are we then to think that all is over because Satan was bound? For instance, are we to think that when this angel took the dragon, the serpent, the devil, and bound him, it was all over and from here on out everything would work smoothly and fine? No. Satan is restrained, and now there is a limit on his activities. The same language and thoughts that imply that God set bounds for the ocean, so that the waves cannot go any further than just so far, hold the same conception that God has set a boundary upon evil. There are certain limits beyond which Satan cannot go, and because of that you and I are safe. He is allowed to tempt us. God will be faithful. He will not suffer us to be tempted beyond what we are able to endure. He will, with the temptation, provide a way of escape that we may be able to bear it. But some people are foolishly going to heed the suggestions of Satan and be deceived by him and maybe taken by him. And that will occur from time to time.

Let me return to the illustration of a vicious dog. We put the dog on a chain and limit the range of his activity. If anyone is foolish enough to get within his reach, that person will be bitten. But a person could stay out of the dog's reach and so would be safe. Now, that is about the way the world is in which we are living today. Satan is active. But the believer in Christ can know that the devil may not touch him. The devil may not touch me. Do you know how I can keep away from him? All I need to do is get into the presence of the Lord Jesus Christ. In His presence the devil has no power.

Now verse 4: "And I saw thrones, and they sat upon them." John does not say here who they were, but later on he does. "And judgment was given unto them: and I saw the souls of them that were beheaded for the witness of Jesus, and for the word of God, and which had not worshipped the beast, neither his image, neither had received his mark upon their foreheads, or in their hands; and they lived and reigned with

Christ a thousand years." These were people who simply had not given themselves over to Satan in any way, shape, or form. They lived and reigned with Christ a thousand years.

It is startling to realize that every single believer is included in this fourth verse. This includes you, if you are a believer in Christ. Every believer is here—you and me. If it is true that He has made us to be kings and priests unto God—a kingdom of priests—then when will we be so? The very language means that He has made us to be a kingdom of priests now. Peter calls us royal priests (see 1 Peter 2:5). Peter asked, "Lord, we have forsaken all and followed thee; what do we get?" Jesus replied, "You will sit upon the twelve thrones, judging the twelve tribes of Israel" (Matt. 19:27-28). I think many of us believers in Christ do not realize that we could have the glory of the Lord now. You and I are to be a kingdom of priests now. In what sense are we to reign? Over ourselves.

We are to be free unto God, bondservants of the Lord Jesus Christ. We sit with Him in heavenly places, and He sits on a throne. We should be conscious of the fact that now in this day and time, we are really blessed by the Lord Jesus Christ, who has given us the opportunity of living in a country where we are free to worship God as we will, and to speak His Word without opposition. We ought to thank Him.

It never has dawned on me so much as in this context that He actually wants me to reign with Him. I should understand the victories that He gives me inwardly over my own selfish disposition and over the circumstances that surround me; every opportunity I have of winning a victory actually is the King's business. When I reflect on this, I realize I ought to act more like the son of a King.

"And I saw thrones, and they sat upon them, and judgment was given unto them: and I saw the souls of them. . . ." I do not think this rule is limited to martyrs. While the description here is of certain martyrs—those who were beheaded for the witness of Jesus—I am not sure that every person had all these characteristics. It would seem to be true if we were to take the group as a whole and think of all believers.

Remember that, in John's day, being a believer was to risk one's life. Being a believer was to be put under pressure to worship the beast—i.e., to worship the Roman Empire, with its emperor. Any believer in Christ in John's time would, I think, recognize himself in this company of people who were endangered because of these things. However, I have no zeal for limiting this passage to martyrs of the first century.

The fact that these persons are sitting on the throne with the Lord reminds me of something that appears all through the New Testament, especially in Paul's Epistles. The Lord Jesus told His disciples that they would sit upon the twelve thrones judging the tribes of Israel (Matt. 19:28). Later on, the apostle Paul would use such language as this, "If we suffer [with him], we shall also reign with him" (2 Tim. 2:12). This is brought out again and again. This matter of reigning with the Lord is held out to be the expectation of all believing people.

"Whosoever will be chief among you, let him be your servant" (Matt. 20:27). I wonder whether the humblest believing woman we have ever seen, who meekly serves, is not the true queen in the situation. I wonder whether or not that faithful believing man that we know of, who steadily, faithfully and humbly serves other people at the cost of self-denial, is not actually a king under God. I wonder if that isn't like the King of Kings and the Lord of all.

THE DEVIL CAST INTO THE LAKE OF FIRE
(Revelation 20:3-10)

> But the rest of the dead lived not again until the thousand years were finished. This is the first resurrection (20:5).

There is a considerable difference of opinion about the resurrection. I have for a long time heard and just naturally supposed that there would be two resurrections after this life. I know that it says that there shall be a resurrection "both of the just and the unjust" (Acts 24:15). But in that particular instance, as Paul says it, it does not say "resurrections"—it does not use the plural. And in my own mind, because of the teaching and training I received, I always took it to mean that there likely would be two—first one and then the other. I know the Bible speaks of a first resurrection, as in this passage. Scripture also speaks of a second resurrection, though the word "second" itself is not used.

What was the first thing that died? When God said, "In the day that thou eatest thereof, dying thou shalt die" (see Gen. 2:17). In what sense is every human being already dead? Is it not that all are dead in trespasses and sins? Every one of us is dead in sin. And is it not true that each believer in Christ, when he is regenerated—born again—is raised with Him in the newness of life? Believers in Christ talk one to another about living in the resurrection power and the resurrection life of the Lord Jesus Christ. Consider that a man has a body and has a soul—there is the spirit of man and there is the body of man—and consider also that as far as his spirit is concerned, it is resurrected at the time that he is born again. Then we understand that the body will be resurrected in the final resurrection, when the body is raised from the dead and the man is presented before God, so that spirit, soul, and body will be preserved blameless in His sight.

With this in mind, those who have had the first resurrection are the regenerated ones. These are the ones whose spirits have been raised from the dead. Every born-again person has this word from God: "Whosoever liveth and believeth in me shall never die" (John 11:26). "I am the resurrection, and the life: he that believeth in me, though he were dead, yet shall he live" (John 11:25; see also John 5:24). Thus the first resurrection can be seen as the resurrection or the regeneration of the spirit. Then the second resurrection will be the resurrection of the body. It seems possible to think of it that way.

Thus we could restate Revelation 20:6: "Blessed and holy is he who has been regenerated, whose spirit has been raised by the power of God through his faith in the Lord Jesus Christ. On such the second death has no power." What is the second death? The death of the body.

The death of the soul—the death of the spirit in sin—occurred when Adam died and death passed upon all men, as Paul said (Rom. 5:12). As a human being, a child of Adam, in my soul and spirit I was dead in the sight of God. My body was still living, but it had the sentence of death upon it and it will die. When we hold the first death to be the death of the soul and spirit in sin, and the second death to be the death of the body, then we can hold the first resurrection to be one's regeneration, and the second resurrection to be the resurrection of one's body, which is what believers in Christ are expecting. We do not think of our spirits as being resurrected in the future because our spirits are regenerated now.

". . . But they shall be priests of God and of Christ, and shall reign with him a thousand years" (Rev. 20:6). Let us remember that by the thousand years we do not mean calendar years; this refers to a vast extent of time as the time that the Lord Jesus Christ will rule. "And when the thousand years are expired, Satan shall be loosed out of his prison" (20:7). After this period of time—during which the Messiah, the Lord Jesus Christ, has bound Satan, restrained him, and didn't kill him, didn't destroy him; and during which the people who believed in Him and did not yield to the earthly powers and influences but were born again and regenerated by God's grace and reigned with Christ—when the time of the gospel age is gone, then the thousand years are expired and Satan is loosed out of his prison.

"He shall go out to deceive the nations which are in the four quarters of the earth, Gog and Magog." I understand that the words Gog and Magog simply refer to earth and kingdom. But no matter what we make of Gog and Magog, John says Satan set out "to deceive the nations which are in the four quarters of the earth." All the nations of the world were "to gather together to battle."

"And they went up on the breadth of the earth, and compassed the camp of the saints about, and the beloved city: and fire came down from God out of heaven, and devoured them." We might notice that these nations surrounded "the camp of the saints." Some people wonder whether the "saints" will be involved in what is here on earth, and this raises a question of identification. As students try to identify who these saints are, it is surprising how well-meaning interpreters identify so many different companies of saints. They have one company of this kind of people and one company of that kind of people, because in that way the saints can fit in with what the interpreters have planned out. In any case, no matter what company they see here, "the saints" are going to be right there at the time of this great battle. And the enemies led by Satan will compass them about as well as the beloved city. The city of God—that is, God's beloved city, which I take to be Jerusalem—will not be taken away at that time.

"And fire came down from God out of heaven, and devoured them." This is a short description of that battle. There isn't much told about what went on; it merely says how they lined up and how it ended. I expect there are other parts of the Book of Revelation that give a much better picture of what is going to happen at that time. It is not going to be easy. It will not be easy for those who belong to the Lord in the day when Satan has persuaded all national leaders to do his will, when all human organizations will be endued with a common spirit of such a nature that they will find themselves opposed to those who simply worship God and not human might. It will not be easy for the believers. Elsewhere in Scripture we are given to understand that this will be such a day that if God did not intervene, the saints would all be exterminated. But however we take it here, God intervened. Fire came down from God and devoured the enemies of His saints.

Compare this passage with Revelation 19:17-21 and note whether this battle referred to in verses 8-9 is not strikingly like what is described there. Note 19:19 to see the similarity. In 19:17 the call was to the fowls to come and gather together "unto the supper of the great God"; that they "may eat the flesh of kings, and the flesh of captains, and the flesh of mighty men, and the flesh of horses, and of them that sit on them, and the flesh of all men, both free and bond, both small and great." Chapter 19 continues, "And I saw the beast, and the kings of the earth, and their armies, gathered together to make war against him that sat on the horse, and against his army." In 19:21 the record of that battle is "And the remnant were slain with the sword of him that sat upon the horse."

Obviously there is a great battle referred to in chapter 19 with the total destruction of the enemy. Here, in chapter 20, we again have a great battle with the total destruction of the enemy. It seems to me that this could well be that great final conflict that will take place between the hosts of God and the hosts of the antichrist, those who are against Him. Earlier than this, we recall the dragon impelled people to make war with the Lamb. I think this is the same. I am inclined to think all these are various views of that final great conflict. What shall we understand is to happen to these people? "Fire came down from God out of heaven. and devoured them. And the devil that deceived them was cast into the lake of fire."

And at the end of chapter 20, John wrote, "And whosoever was not found written in the book of life was cast into the lake of fire." Fire is associated with that event, and the only thing I can say is that this is the last we will hear of it.

THE GREAT WHITE THRONE
(Revelation 20:11-15)

Verse 11 of chapter 20 introduces another scene in John's vision. This is the only place in Scripture where there is reference to "the great white throne." The judgment at the great white throne does not come until the conclusion of all these events on earth.

Jesus of Nazareth taught about the wheat and the tares: "Let them both grow together until the harvest." The harvest will come. In Matthew 13 He said the harvest is the end of the world. The harvest will come. And at that time, God will gather the wheat together into the granary, and the chaff and the tares will be burned with fire. There will be this sifting process: this great white throne is the winnowing. We now see here in Revelation 20 how it will happen.

> And I saw a great white throne, and him that sat on it, from whose face the earth and the heaven fled away; and there was found no place for them. And I saw the dead, small and great, stand before God; and the books were opened: and another book was opened, which is the book of life (20:11-12).

Let us take a good look at this, because here is where our salvation is secure. It is not too clearly seen in these two verses but in subsequent chapters it is plain that these people whose names were written in the Lamb's book of life would never come before the great white throne. That great white throne is the judgment seat, a courtroom seat. All the accused, all mankind, both small and great, were all there before God. And the books were opened, as if every man had his time with God to give an account for the deeds done in the body, and to give an account for every idle word spoken.

Then there is another book opened, a little book off to one side. It has some names in it. These are the names of persons who have settled out of court. They came in ahead of time and pleaded guilty, and God dealt with them. That is where my name is. I have been in before the Lord, and I pleaded guilty. He paid my fine: the blood of the Lord Jesus Christ has cleansed me from every sin. And thanks be to almighty God; I can say, "Praise His holy name." I will never stand before that throne to be judged for my sins. Unworthy as I am—so that I never will be able to praise Him adequately—I will never have to appear before that throne. Because I have been to Him, my judgment is passed. There is no condemnation to those who are in Christ Jesus (Rom. 8:1). No judgment awaits those persons whose names are in the Lamb's book of life. "He that . . . believeth on him that sent me, . . . shall not come into condemnation; but is passed from death unto life" (John 5:24). If you are a believer, your name is written in the little book, and you will never stand before that throne.

> . . . And the dead were judged out of those things which were written in the books, according to their works. And the sea gave up the dead which were in it; and death and hell delivered up the dead which were in them: and they were judged every man according to their works. And death and hell were cast into the lake of fire. This is the second death. And whosoever was not found written in the book of life was cast into the lake of fire (20:12-15).

This is a passage we can scarcely read and think about without having great sorrow of heart. The only thing we can trust at this time is the righteousness and the mercy of God. We can remember that God Himself gave His Son. His invitation was open to all people. He has called again and again and patiently waited. There cannot be a wider, more generous invitation than "Come unto me, all ye that labour and are heavy laden, and I will give you rest" (Matt. 11:28).

Chapters 21 and 22

† † †

NEW HEAVEN AND NEW EARTH
(Revelation 21:1-3)

As we come to chapter 21 of Revelation, something is seen that we have been waiting for—something that the human heart waits for anytime it looks into the face of God and thinks about the universe. Anytime we think about life we want what John saw here:

> And I saw a new heaven and a new earth: for the first heaven and the first earth were passed away; and there was no more sea (21:1).

For the first time, it is different than it has ever been up until now. The Greek word for "new" does not imply a different other heaven, but a renewed heaven. The first heaven and the first earth—the way in which things were with sin in them—were passed away and there was no more sea. Now I think that, generally speaking, for many of us the phrase "there was no more sea" is passed by simply as a poetic expression. But we might in recalling Scripture carry in mind that the sea is associated with several things.

The sea separates. Between the nations in John's day lay the sea. And the sea was a separation. The people who lived beyond the seas and the islands of seas were at a distance. And even with us today, the sea is the great separator. We think about the river that separates us from the people on the other side. And when we say, "There was no more sea" we may say, "No more separation." That will be a good thing to say: free access coming and going. In this new heaven and new earth, no more separation.

It was out of the sea that the beast came that was such an

enemy of the land and who did so much damage and caused so much distress and persecution and suffering. The beast came out of the sea. Now the sea is gone. There will be no more evil principle originating to disturb and to distress mankind. And then again, we will remember that back in the Old Testament it speaks about wickedness being like the waters of the troubled seas, casting up mire and dirt (Isa. 57:20). There was no more sea. For Satan is destroyed. John has seen that the ultimate end of Satan and of all evil is that they will be destroyed. And now he is given an insight to see what happens when that evil is gone. When Satan has been destroyed and when the very source of evil is gone, than what? There is no more source of evil, no more restlessness. It is all gone. The troubled sea is no more.

> And I John saw the holy city, new Jerusalem, coming down from God out of heaven, prepared as a bride adorned for her husband (21:2).

Let us contrast this scene with Babel: that wicked city, Babel and Babylon, that mother of harlots, that source of all abomination; the culmination of human pride, human effort, and human interest. We remember how it was when the men of Babel said, "Go to, let us build, let us make us something. Something that will reach up into heaven. We human beings will get this thing done" (see Gen. 11). But there is a contrast here. When John writes in 21:2 that the holy city is coming down from God out of heaven, we are not to think that this is an event of history. This does not mean that after all evil has been destroyed, then the holy city comes down out of heaven. Rather, with the evil gone, attention is now focused upon the holy city.

This expression "coming down out of heaven" is not a matter of history and time, it is a matter of origin. This city comes from God. The Scripture records that Abraham looked for a city, whose Maker and Builder is God (Heb. 11:10). Here John sees this holy city coming down from God out of heaven "prepared as a bride adorned for her husband." In this one paragraph, different figures are used to refer to that city. It is a holy city. It is Jerusalem. It is a bride. And all these are figures of speech which indicate the intent of God.

> And I heard a great voice out of heaven saying, Behold, the
> tabernacle of God is with men, and he will dwell with them,
> and they shall be his people, and God himself shall be with
> them, and be their God (21:3).

In the Old Testament it was revealed that this is what God
started out to show the world in Israel. When He called the
Hebrews out of Egypt and had them build the tabernacle, He
then gave them instructions on how to live clean lives, because He was going to be in their midst. And He said, "I will
be their God and they shall be my people" (see Lev. 26:12).
Paul cites Old Testament passages when he writes, "Come
out from among them, and be ye separate, saith the
Lord. . . . and I will receive you, and will be a Father unto
you, and ye shall be my sons and daughters, saith the Lord
Almighty" (2 Cor. 6:17-18). This is the same thought. God will
dwell in the midst of His people, and God will be with them
and He will be their God.

THE GLORIOUS INVITATION
(Revelation 21:4–22:21)

> And God shall wipe away all tears from their eyes; and there
> shall be no more death, neither sorrow, nor crying, neither
> shall there be any more pain: for the former things are passed
> away (21:4).

There will be no more tears. "The former things are passed
away"—the things that were in the flesh, in sin. Just as long as
there are human beings with sin, there will be tears, and they
will be shed. Jesus of Nazareth shed tears over Jerusalem.

    Just as long as there is sin, human beings will die: the wages
of sin is death. And just as long as there are human beings in
their natural selves, there is going to be sorrow. Even Jesus of
Nazareth was "a man of sorrows, and acquainted with grief"
(Isa. 53:3). As long as human beings are as they are, there will
be crying and there will be pain—real pain. But when God
wipes away all tears from their eyes and there is no more

death, neither sorrow nor crying, neither any more pain, then will be the new heaven and the new earth, where the former things are passed away, and where there is left no more sea.

> And he that sat upon the throne said, Behold, I make all things new. And he said unto me, Write: for these words are true and faithful (21:5).

God started making things new when we became believers in Christ. Every man in Christ Jesus is a new creation. We ought to tell one another more often that we who believe in the Lord Jesus Christ and have experienced God's regenerating work are the firstfruits of a new creation. We are in this world like pioneers, not so much of a new world here, as of a new world later when the Lord completes His will. But we belong to that other world now; our citizenship is in heaven. In this world we are strangers and pilgrims acting as ambassadors of that heavenly city. We belong there, so we are here only as strangers and pilgrims. Believers in Christ are interested in people. They are trying to help people. May God give us the insight to see that the only way to help the human being, so the human heart can ever be satisfied, is to bring it into that fellowship with God wherein it is not limited to time and space and to the things of this earth.

The heart of the believer is brought into the heavenly things about which we are thinking. Believers in Christ who have conscious spiritual experience get glimmerings of this. I wonder if there is any believer in Christ who has not had some blessed experience of God's having wiped away the tears from his eyes. "I make all things new."

"And he said unto me, Write: for these words are true and faithful." The reader could put a punctuation period right at the end of this verse. This is the culmination of what the Lord Jesus Christ has to say. So far as the rest of the Book of Revelation is concerned, we may get some amplifications of this, but we will find nothing unique.

Revelation 21:3-4 describes the very essence of heaven. The believer in Christ will be in the presence of God, and God will be with him. God will share every burden he has, and God will carry every load he has. And as long as the believer in Christ lives, whether it be on earth or in heaven, he will be living with God. When a person realizes that, he will be walking in heaven. So in this world he will look upon people as the people whom God made. And it will be surprising what a love there will be in his heart toward all human beings. This will be not because he is human, and not because he is nice, and not because he is wicked, and not because he is pitiable, and not because he feels sorry for them; but because they belong to God.

The old-time religion makes us love everybody. It will just come out of us and spread over them. And it will lift us. And in the ordinary experiences of living in this world, the sorrows and griefs that come cannot last. They will be like snowflakes falling onto a hot stove: they will simply melt away. Hurtful experiences will not stay. The believer in Christ will be an amazement to everyone else because of the quietness and the peace that he will have.

"And he said unto me, It is done . . ." (21:6). I am sure you recognize that word "It is done." That is the word Christ spoke from the cross. Remember when He said that? "Finished"—it is the same word. In Revelation 16:17 John writes that when the angel poured out the seventh vial of God's wrath, he said, "It is done." And here the message comes to John from the Lord, "It is done."

> And he said unto me, It is done. I am Alpha and Omega, the beginning and the end. I will give unto him that is athirst of the fountain of the water of life freely (21:6).

This is the Lord Jesus Christ saying to John there on the Isle of Patmos, "I have shown you these things. And I am the beginning and the end. All things are in me."

When we read through the rest of this chapter and then through chapter 22, we come to the most wonderful invitation I have ever heard. In the latter part of chapter 22 it will be the same as this: "Let him that is athirst come." For every creature, every Bible-class teacher, every personal worker, everyone who understands the gospel, this is the most wonderful promise we will ever hear. All in the world that is needed is for people to be hungry; the gospel is the food. All in the world that is needed is for them to be thirsty; there is an absolutely assured source, a fountain of living water, for them. We can promise "Blessed are they which do hunger and thirst after righteousness: for they shall be filled" (Matt. 5:6). God is

alive! God is watching over people. And the hungry heart He
will not forsake. He will stay with the thirsty soul.

> He that overcometh shall inherit all things; and I will be his
> God, and he shall be my son (21:7).

In chapters 2 and 3, which record messages sent to the seven
churches, you will recall how after He had told each church
what to do He told them "he that overcometh shall have this"
and "he that overcometh shall have that." He said this seven
different times. Here it is again: "He that overcometh shall
inherit all things": all seven of them. He will have it all. "I will
be his God, and he shall be my son." The believer in Christ
can be sure he has graduated; there just isn't any more. That
is the whole business. He will belong to God.

> But the fearful, and unbelieving, and the abominable, and
> murderers, and whoremongers, and sorcerers, and idolaters,
> and all liars, shall have their part in the lake which burneth
> with fire and brimstone (21:8).

"But the fearful"—that is to say, the people who in looking
out on things are moved by fear and not by faith, the people
whose hearts are gripped with apprehension, not with
confidence. This verse, as it categorizes people, does not
mean that at this point such persons are put away, because we
remember that actually in chapter 20 they were put away,
"which is the second death."

> And there came unto me one of the seven angels which had the
> seven vials full of the seven last plagues, and talked with me,
> saying, Come hither, I will show thee the bride, the Lamb's
> wife (21:9).

The bride was mentioned earlier in verse 2, but now an angel
says to John, "Come hither, I will show thee the bride."

> And he carried me away in the spirit to a great and high moun-
> tain, and showed me that great city, the holy Jerusalem, de-
> scending out of heaven from God, having the glory of God: and
> her light was like unto a stone most precious, even like a jasper
> stone, clear as crystal; and had a wall great and high, and had
> twelve gates, and at the gates twelve angels, and names written
> thereon, which are the names of the twelve tribes of the chil-
> dren of Israel: on the east three gates; on the north three gates;
> on the south three gates; and on the west three gates
> (21:10-13).

The contrast with the true Jerusalem would be the gate. The earthly Jerusalem had only a few gates (see Neh. 12:31-39); the heavenly Jerusalem has twelve gates. The earthly Jerusalem was so constructed as to keep people out; this heavenly Jerusalem is so constructed as to let people in, from all sides.

> And the wall of the city had twelve foundations, and in them the names of the twelve apostles of the Lamb (21:14).

This is interesting, for here we find John blending again the twelve tribes of Israel in the Old Testament and the twelve apostles of the New Testament.

> And he that talked with me had a golden reed to measure the city, and the gates thereof, and the wall thereof. And the city lieth foursquare, and the length is as large as the breadth: and he measured the city with the reed, twelve thousand furlongs. The length and the breadth and the height of it are equal (21:15-16).

It is calculated in research that twelve thousand furlongs is about fourteen hundred miles. "The length and the breadth and the height of it are equal," so the city is a cube. But we need always to keep in mind that any measurement of space or time is only symbolic in a vision.

> And he measured the wall thereof, an hundred and forty and four cubits, according to the measure of man, that is, of the angel. And the building of the wall of it was of jasper: and the city was pure gold, like unto clear glass (21:17-18).

Now, gold is not like clear glass, but if we take a diamond and then pure gold polished brightly and then transparent glass, each of these things would be bright, glorious, impressive.

> And the foundations of the wall of the city were garnished with all manner of precious stones . . . (21:19).

John writes as though he had stepped into a jewelry store. Twelve different precious stones, as they were called at that time, are named. The impression given is of something of value, rare and exquisitely beautiful.

> And the twelve gates were twelve pearls: every several gate was of one pearl . . . (21:21).

From this verse comes the expression "the pearly gate." Each gate was a pearl. Pearls were very precious.

> . . . and the street of the city was pure gold, as it were transparent glass (21:21).

What we are to understand here is that this thing which God does—this solution that God offers to living, this arrangement of all living relationships that God would have in His will—is pure and magnificent and glorious. That is the impression being made on us.

> And I saw no temple therein: for the Lord God Almighty and the Lamb are the temple of it. And the city had no need of the sun, neither of the moon, to shine in it: for the glory of God did lighten it, and the Lamb is the light thereof. And the nations of them which are saved shall walk in the light of it: and the kings of the earth do bring their glory and honour into it. And the gates of it shall not be shut at all by day: for there shall be no night there. And they shall bring the glory and honour of the nations into it. And there shall in no wise enter into it any thing that defileth, neither whatsoever worketh abomination, or maketh a lie: but they which are written in the Lamb's book of life. And he showed me a pure river of water of life, clear as crystal, proceeding out of the throne of God and of the Lamb (21:22–22:1).

We recognize again how figurative this is. We do not have a river coming out of a throne in actual physical life. But we have the relationship. This river of the water of life flowing from the very authority of God, by the very sovereignty of God, out of the throne of God and the Lamb.

> In the midst of the street of it, and on either side of the river, was there the tree of life . . . (22:2).

Here is another instance where we cannot interpret the scene literally: it would be very awkward and irrational to have a river flowing with a tree growing on both sides of it, one tree.

> In the midst of the street of it, and on either side of the river, was there the tree of life, which bare twelve manner of fruits, and yielded her fruit every month: and the leaves of the tree were for the healing of the nations (22:2).

The tree of life stood in the Garden of Eden. Genesis begins with it and Revelation ends with it. In the last chapter of Revelation there are more references to the first two chapters of Genesis than there are anywhere else in the Bible. The Bible begins in Genesis 1 and 2 and ends in Revelation 21 and

22. And it is amazing how many things that were opened and broken in Genesis 1–3 are brought together and made perfect in Revelation 21 and 22.

> And there shall be no more curse . . . (22:3).

The curse was introduced to the universe back in Genesis 3. But now there will be a curse no more.

> . . . But the throne of God and of the Lamb shall be in it; and his servants shall serve him: and they shall see his face; and his name shall be in their foreheads (22:3-4).

"No more curse" means that the earth will not bring forth briars and thorns. It means that man will not be hindered and hampered in his work so that he will have to eat his bread in the sweat of his brow; the woman will not be having sorrow and distress and agony all her days; Satan will not be active to hurt and to bruise the heel of the seed of the woman. There will be no more curse. All the tension and the contention and the conflict are gone in this situation.

"And his servants shall serve him: and they shall see his face." This will be the total, perfect joy. You and I at this distance can only hear about it and imagine it. And the best thing I can suggest, when we wonder what it would be like to see His face, is to have us consider it from a human point of view. Can we remember a time when we were in love? Was there any sweeter joy than to look into the face of the person we loved? We may count on it that heaven is an unbroken extension to the "nth" degree of that forever. The hymn expresses it for us: "O that will be glory for me." These servants that serve Him shall see His face. "And his name shall be in their foreheads": they will be as surely identified with Him as the unbelievers were identified with the beast (13:16).

> And there shall be no night there; and they need no candle, neither light of the sun; for the Lord God giveth them light: and they shall reign for ever and ever. And he said unto me, These sayings are faithful and true: and the Lord God of the holy prophets sent his angel to show unto his servants the things which must shortly be done. Behold, I come quickly: blessed is he that keepeth the sayings of the prophecy of this book (22:5-7).

We can close this here. The message is complete. John has only a few more things to say to us.

> And I John saw these things, and heard them. And when I had heard and seen, I fell down to worship before the feet of the angel which showed me these things. Then saith he unto me, See thou do it not: for I am thy fellow-servant, and of thy brethren the prophets, and of them which keep the sayings of this book: worship God (22:8-9).

If we cherish these things, we are like the prophets and like John in the sight of God. We are like the angels. God will accept us, if we cherish these things and hold them to our hearts. John ends verse 9 with a clear statement of ultimate truth: "Worship God." No one else, nothing else.

> And he saith unto me, Seal not the sayings of the prophecy of this book: for the time is at hand (22:10).

In other words, John is not to keep this secret. He is to let it out, let people know about it.

> He that is unjust, let him be unjust still: and he which is filthy, let him be filthy still: and he that is righteous, let him be righteous still: and he that is holy, let him be holy still (22:11).

What has been done here on earth is done. It is done. Here on earth the battle is decided. If we have accepted the Lord Jesus Christ, we are saved. If we reject the Lord Jesus Christ, we are lost. It is over. Whatsoever we bind on earth is bound in heaven; whatsoever we loose on earth is loosed in heaven (Matt. 18:18). The whole business down here in this world matters. It matters eternally what you and I do with God, and with the Lord Jesus Christ in serving Him.

> And, behold, I come quickly: and my reward is with me, to give every man according as his work shall be (22:12).

This saying "He comes quickly" does not mean Christ comes with great speed. It means He comes suddenly. He will come unexpectedly. He will come without fanfare. In other places the Scriptures say He will come like a thief in the night (1 Thess. 5:2; 2 Peter 3:10). He will be there. "And my reward is with me, to give every man according as his work shall be."

> I am Alpha and Omega, the beginning and the end, the first and the last. Blessed are they that do his commandments, that

> they may have right to the tree of life, and may enter in through the gates into the city (22:13-14).

We might ask what would be the doing of His commandments? It begins with our believing in the Lord Jesus Christ. When our Lord Jesus was here on earth, the people asked Him, "What shall we do that we might work the works of God?" He said, "This is the work of God, that ye believe on him whom he hath sent" (John 6:28-29). Now what this means is that we believe on Christ, whom God the Father sent. It means we commit ourselves to Him in service, in His will, in His name, and yield ourselves to Him and let His will be done in us. That is what this means.

> For without are dogs, and sorcerers, and whoremongers, and murderers, and idolaters, and whosoever loveth and maketh a lie. I Jesus have sent mine angel to testify unto you these things in the churches. I am the root and the offspring of David, and the bright and morning star. And the Spirit and the bride say, Come . . . (22:15-17).

I have moved quickly to this point, because this is what I earlier called the greatest invitation I know in the Bible. Look at it:

> And the Spirit and the bride say, Come. And let him that heareth say, Come. And let him that is athirst come. And whosoever will, let him take the water of life freely (22:17).

This is the great invitation!

> For I testify unto every man that heareth the words of the prophecy of this book, If any man shall add unto these things, God shall add unto him the plagues that are written in this book: and if any man shall take away from the words of the book of this prophecy, God shall take away his part out of the book of life, and out of the holy city, and from the things which are written in this book. He which testifieth these things saith, Surely I come quickly. Amen. Even so, come, Lord Jesus. The grace of our Lord Jesus Christ be with you all. Amen (22:18-21).

This was John's prayer, "Even so, come, Lord Jesus." It is my prayer. And then the benediction: "The grace of our Lord Jesus Christ be with you all. Amen." It is my benediction too.